Planagement®–
Moving Concept into
Reality

Planagement® — Moving Concept into Reality

Planagement is registered as a trademark and a service mark with the U.S. Patent Office.

ROBERT M. RANDOLPH

Planagement is registered as a trademark and a service mark with the U.S. Patent Office.

Library of Congress Cataloging in Publication Data

Randolph, Robert M   1934–
  Planagement: moving concept into reality.

  Bibliography: p.
  1. Management.   I.   Title.
HD31.R27   1979   658.4   79-17075
ISBN 0-89384-056-4

Learning Concepts
2501 North Lamar
Austin, Texas 78705

First – Fourth Printings — AMACOM
Fifth Printing, July 1979 — Learning Concepts

Jacket Design by
  Gretchen Reed and
  Suzanne Pustejovsky

Foreword

As I READ this book, I had the distinctly pleasurable feeling that here is something good for the manager and for other people—something good, useful, and very much needed.

The author and I have worked together many times and have collaborated in many ways. He is one of the relatively few (but rapidly increasing) professionals who see management as more than a craft, more than a science—rather, as an art.

One of the principal ways in which this is manifested is his recognition that the dream and the reality of significant undertakings are indivisible.

His treatment of "Concepts" is fully in accord with the tough-minded axiom that "concepts are the stuff of wisdom, and wisdom is the stuff of management." A management dream is not viable without muscle, e.g., processes, procedures, systems, and policies. At the same time, such nitty-gritty items cannot be truly viable without the transcendent stretch of the big picture, the grand design, the *dream*.

He has wasted no time in tight-lipped, downbeat thinking. He offers instead a way to go, to move, to grow. He is to be commended for this.

Accordingly, I take deep pleasure in recommending this stimulating book to all who wish to strive for greater daily effectiveness and joy.

Joe D. Batten

Preface

THIS BOOK will introduce you to a system that is being used to considerable advantage by several thousand people and many organizations, large and small, profit and nonprofit—the Planagement® System. It has been reviewed and tested by managers, educators, consultants, psychologists, trainers, and motivators. The general consensus is that while many of its elements are not new and have frequently been written about, the Planagement System is unique because of the way it has combined many old and new ideas into an approach that increases their understanding and practical use. In addition, applying the Planagement System produces measurable results—primarily because the best concepts and ideas, which are normally fragmented, have been integrated into a single, teachable, total management system supported by practical and productive tools.

What is Planagement? As a formal definition, it is a process that integrates the art and science of converting a concept into reality through the use of a practiced method. In practical terms, it is a system that combines the concepts of planning with the realities of operating management. The system provides a constructive blend of

Planagement is registered as a trademark and a service mark with the U.S. Patent Office.

scientific management and the behavioral sciences. And, more than anything else, Planagement is a method for increasing individual and management effectiveness. This teachable, systematic skill for planning/management/communication/motivation/development/and control assists each individual to do more, in less time, with better results.

Because Planagement adapts to the individual, it is universally applicable to organizations of various sizes, structures, and purposes, as well as to all levels and functions of management. The Planagement System may also be applied to programs, projects, individual jobs, and to individuals themselves.

This book has been designed to serve those individuals and organizations that are committed to constantly improving their present situation while mastering the self-discipline required for the pursuit of excellence and the achievement of potential. The Planagement System was created for them, and it is to these soundly growing individuals and organizations that this book is dedicated.

Robert M. Randolph

Contents

Part I

The Need

1

The Present Situation

How WELL do you know your own potential? Granted, this is not an easy question to answer, yet it is a vitally important one. If a person does not understand his potential, then obviously he cannot manage that potential in the best way. Very few people have given much consideration to their own potential, and as a result less than 5 percent consider themselves successful as measured by their ability to live up to their own capabilities and achieve the objectives they have set for themselves.

To objectively test your own insight into your potential, ask yourself these questions:

- Do you have a written plan for your future that includes your most important objectives in order of priority?
- Do you have an identifiable method for planning, both long-term and daily? Could you easily teach this method to someone else?
- Do you have a written checklist for making sound decisions? Can it be used successfully in any situation?
- Do you have a system to do more, in less time, with better results? Could you teach this system to someone else?
- Do you understand the step-by-step process of common sense? How many steps are there, and could you write them down on

a piece of paper so that someone else could use them to advantage?
- What is your most important capability?
- Where does your most important potential lie? What percentage of your total potential do you feel you are reaching? How do you plan to achieve more of your unrealized potential?

How well did you do in answering these questions? The answers frequently determine a person's future success, yet probably less than 2 percent of the population can answer more than a couple of these questions in a positive way, which means that 90 percent must have their work planned for them and need supervision to accomplish the plan, and 8 percent will do only a part of their planning and require some supervision to get their job done. The elite 2 percent who have developed the capability to plan their lives and their work and to accomplish their plan without supervision are usually the unquestioned leaders in their chosen fields. These rare individuals achieve considerable success and satisfaction from what they do.

Perhaps the most important factor that separates these few leaders from the others is that they have developed a skill that allows them to consistently manage inconsistent situations so that they produce constant gain. This skill is built on their most important capability and aimed directly at realizing their own potential.

The Process of Common Sense

Why don't more people develop such a skill? It is not because they would not like to, but rather because they do not know how to soundly plan, manage, and control their lives. They do not understand the process of common sense—the method for making practical and reasonable decisions. This was clearly recognized by Emerson when he observed that "the trouble with common sense is that it is too uncommon."

Because so few people use their common sense to advantage, most lives, both individual and organizational, are lived without a clearly defined direction and supporting plan. This unfortunate situation can be compared to working a jigsaw puzzle without the picture and with all the pieces the same color. Those who lack direction take a lot longer to fit their irreplaceable pieces of time into a meaningful picture of where their lives are heading. Eventually they—and their organizations—end up managing their own mediocre momentum and allowing changes to manage them, whether those changes are bad or good.

These people seem to have the time to do only what is necessary, not what is desirable. Since they do not do things right in the first place because they do not know how to do them right in the first place, they must spend time doing them over.

The Challenge of Change

People fear the future and are resistant to change because they lack direction and are unable to manage change. This state of mind is extremely dangerous to individuals as well as to organizations because we live in an age in which change is the only constant. And there are only three things we know for sure about the future:

The future will not be like the past.
The future will not be what we think it's going to be.
The rate of change will be faster than ever before.

As individuals, and collectively in organizations, we are subject to revolutionary changes in technology, economics, government, and social attitudes.

These revolutions have introduced a frighteningly rapid obsolescence of ideas, services, products, and practices. If it's true, as some leading management authorities have stated, that 80 percent of today's management practices are obsolete, then today's prime management challenge is to develop individual and organizational capabilities to manage a rapidly changing external environment.

Alvin Toffler, in his bestseller *Future Shock,** stated that "unless man quickly learns to control the rate of change in his personal affairs as well as in society at large, we are doomed to a massive adaptational breakdown." It would seem that, in addition to controlling the rate of change, man must learn how to favorably influence the direction of change. In other words, we may well be at one of the most critical crossroads in man's history, and our very destiny probably depends on whether we can successfully develop the skill to manage change rather than continuing to allow change to manage us.

There are many reasons why we now find ourselves surrounded by a variety of revolutions. Some of the more important ones are:

1. The population explosion: Even if we maintain our present

* New York: Random House, 1970.

low birth rate, it will be some time before the population begins to level off. Meanwhile we will have to contend with the problems of pollution and allocation of scarcer resources among a still expanding population. At this time, over half of the United States population is twenty-six years of age or younger.

2. The knowledge explosion: If you were to compare all the knowledge accumulated before 1970 to knowledge growth after 1970, you would discover that it has been doubling every two and one-half years, and by the end of 1975 it will be doubling every three and one-half months. Put in other terms, data, the byproduct of knowledge, are being expressed in some form of 500,000 pages of new information every minute.

3. The education explosion: An increasing number of people are receiving more education. This is startlingly illustrated by the fact that 90 percent of the scientists who ever lived are alive today. These trained agents of change contribute in large measure to our dynamic environment, and their expanding skills are being supported by larger allocations of money for research and development.

The primary need in this age of change is to develop a method for managing change that capitalizes on the abundant potential of our environment. Although many people sense this need, most have not developed a method for managing change and are therefore in danger of becoming obsolete. In business circles they are frequently referred to as "obsolete managers," and these turned-off, tuned-out people are part of a growing majority that constitutes private enterprise's most serious vulnerability.

The Obsolete Manager

Who is the obsolete manager? What are his characteristics? Are there many obsolete managers in American industry? What makes the manager obsolete, and how can he reestablish himself as an effective producer? These are the questions most frequently asked when the problem of the obsolete manager is discussed.

The subject of personal obsolesence is a touchy one. Many good people teeter precariously on the ragged edge of complacency and are satisfied to manage momentum rather than potential. In order not to rock the boat, the manager riding the downside of his own demise adopts the motto: My job is not to run the train / Or even clang the bell / But watch the train as it jumps the tracks / And see who catches hell.

Touchy or not, the problem of the obsolete manager must be

objectively faced, compassionately understood, and empathetically dealt with. If organizations do not have this strength, then they will become custodians of their own demise.

Who is the obsolete manager? He is the manager who was born in 1920, died in 1965, and won't be buried until 1980. He is no longer growing and perceives challenge as a threat rather than an opportunity. He doesn't like himself, hates his job, and is convinced there is a vast conspiracy dedicated to making waves in his sea of complacency. While he might agree that 80 percent of today's management practices are obsolete, he is content to leave the problem to those "young bucks" who will take over when he retires.

What are some of his characteristics?

1. His predictions of the future are based only on past experiences, and he manages momentum, not potential. He has run out of challenges and is frustrated because he has not been able to establish new and self-actualizing objectives.

2. He concentrates on weaknesses rather than on strengths— he knows what's wrong, not what's right—and this negative attitude makes him a pessimist who sees the difficulty in every opportunity rather than the opportunity in every difficulty. He is also defensive and unable to identify a direction for himself that would improve his unhappy situation.

3. This manager makes the simple seem complex, attempts to make himself indispensable, and won't delegate authority to others.

4. He judges people by their traits and actions rather than by the results they obtain. He is inclined to emphasize *know-who* much more than *know-how*.

5. He relies on numbers and data rather than on people. Since he doesn't believe in people (usually he thinks the behavioral sciences are a lot of "academic nonsense"), he is more of an exploiter than a builder. He trusts no one and considers personal survival the most important law.

6. This type of manager is a poor communicator and thus is constantly misunderstood. He is an anxious talker and a poor listener.

7. Mr. Obsolete is afraid of enthusiasm and extensively uses sarcasm or cynicism to dampen it. He takes credit but rarely gives it, and he is usually against an idea that was "not invented here."

8. The basic strategy of this inept individual is to *get*. He prides himself on getting the best deal, rather than a fair deal. He knows more answers than questions, and he depends on the right to hire and fire for his authority rather than on earned prestige.

9. He manipulates people and prides himself on being an excellent politician. The other guy is the competition who may be after his job, so it becomes a business game to "get him first."

10. He frequently procrastinates rather than make a decision he will be held responsible for.

11. The obsolete manager is more conscious of position and activity than of direction and results. The *how* is emphasized, not the *why*.

12. Frequently his approach is to establish a budget first, and then develop the plan the budget is supposed to support. Functional thinking is more pronounced than profit thinking.

13. He resists change, new ideas, and orderly procedures, and tends to avoid establishing proper policies, procedures, and paperwork.

14. The obsolete manager is pragmatic, dictatorial, and inflexible. He dislikes the participative management approach and is extremely protective of his prerogatives. To him, it is more important to establish his point than to find the truth or the best answer. He manages by his objectives and all others are subordinate.

15. This type of manager will not lead by example; his philosophy is "Do as I say, not as I do." He is disorganized, escapist, and undisciplined. He has no physical fitness program and rarely feels better than adequate. He lacks direction and priorities, and his judgments depend almost entirely on past experience, intuition, and emotion rather than on a balance between these important elements and a logical and factual approach.

Are there many obsolete managers in American industry? Unhappily, the answer is yes. When members of groups composed of managers, industrial psychologists, management educators, writers, consultants, and people engaged in management recruitment were requested to independently write down their estimate of how many United States managers in their thirties, forties, and fifties are obsolete, the answers were within 5 percent of each other. The number of obsolete managers in their thirties was established as 45 to over 50 percent; in their forties, 55 to 60 percent; and in their fifties, over 60 percent. Perhaps this is the same phenomenon observed by Dr. Peter when he stated in his now famous Peter Principle that everybody is destined to rise to his own level of incompetence.

The greatest danger to private enterprise may be that we have created a situation that produces a high number of obsolete managers who go home and tell their children how horrible their job and company are. Consequently, their children passionately reject the so-called establishment, and our hope for future improvement in the situation is in serious jeopardy.

External Environment

There is probably no one answer to what makes so many managers obsolete, but basically it lies in the individual himself and his relationship to his external environment. The business executive is influenced by his job, the climate of his organization, and his own needs (the order of these priorities varies with the individual). A job is based on the needs of the organization, with little consideration given to the needs of the individual. The structure is task-oriented, and results are usually measured by the unclear and subjective standards of a superior.

In every organization there is a hierarchy of jobs, and the emphasis is on advancing in the hierarchy rather than on matching individual needs and skills with a job's requirements. This causes people to compete for the "next job up"—whether or not they are right for it or would be happy in it. Usually the higher the job in the organization structure, the higher the compensation and prestige. Ambition becomes a matter of position, not direction, a game of approved activity rather than of measured results.

Often the lead salesman—who loves to sell—is made a regional or general sales manager and given a higher salary based on his alleged promotion. If the salesman is ambitious, flexible, and desires the additional money and better title, he will attempt to adjust to the managerial requirements of the job. These requirements are very different from what he is used to, and if he does not make a successful adjustment, he will probably be unhappy and fearful for his job. This insecurity will intensify and it soon will be observed that "poor Jack had it at one time, but he was promoted to his level of incompetence and is now obsolete."

The horrible part of Jack's dilemma is that he is trapped by an increased standard of living based on a job he dislikes and a title that has become the measure of his success. Ironically, he may be contributing less to the company's profit than he did when he was breaking sales records—but then, organizations often pay more according to job classification than to the value of results. After all, the name of the game is to advance to a bigger job—like it or not.

This brings us to the second dimension of the external environment that contributes to the creation of the obsolete manager. In some ways, it is a more negative influence than the hierarchy of jobs.

This dimension involves the organization's climate, which is determined by the style and competence of the manager or managers in charge of the company.

Is the climate one of pessimism or optimism? Are ideas welcomed, considered, and decided on—or are they frequently squelched, ignored, or received with a sarcastic "What are you doing, bucking for a promotion?"

Is there an *esprit de corps* based on an understood direction? Or is the climate one of no direction where people have little understanding of the purpose of their work and of the company and consequently regard their jobs merely as something that has to be done to earn a living?

Who sets objectives? On what basis are results measured, or are results measured at all? If not, then working will be about as much fun and offer as much challenge as playing golf with no rules and no par.

Do communications *always* flow down, even though it is recognized that 90 percent of the ideas for growth and development flow up?

Do the people in top management really want to hear the truth? Is the climate one of candor and a common search for the best answer, or is it one where the most popular answer is easily accepted? A cardinal principle of communication is that it must be based on integrity. If you do not believe what I say, then you won't *hear* what I say. You will second-guess me, and we will not communicate. This kind of distrust generates a climate that allows two sets of books: the ones we ourselves use and the ones we give to management and the home office. Of course, once management catches on to the game and starts juggling the information it receives, it will make arbitrary decisions based on inaccurate data—which only compounds the problem of communication and productive personal relationships.

Finally, is the climate one that dictates "right or wrong, the boss is right"? Do the key managers and those who are considered "good corporate men" have the characteristics of the obsolete manager? If so, then the organization will probably attract and tolerate obsolete managers who value their jobs more than they value themselves. These managers will become members of that silent, complacent majority that accepts obsolescence as an established standard in order to survive in an organization climate that has killed them as productive individuals and destroyed their pride in themselves, their work, and their company.

The third dimension of the environment that has an impact on the individual is his own needs. If he tolerates a job he doesn't enjoy and doesn't do well, he will be susceptible to being dominated by the organization's climate—which probably is the negative kind or it would not cause or tolerate the mismatch between the man's needs and skills and the requirements of the job and the organization. Whenever this mismatch is allowed, the individual's primary need will be to survive in what he probably refers to as "the corporate jungle," and his only solace will be the thought that he is providing a good living for his family and someday will be able to retire from the jungle—if he is lucky and keeps his nose clean.

There are, no doubt, additional dimensions and reasons that contribute to creating the obsolete manager; however, the important point is to appraise the situation objectively and evaluate its cost against the cost of taking positive action to turn the situation around. I maintain that we all have the capability to turn the situation around, for ourselves and for our organization, because there is a sound, tangible process that everyone can use to manage change to his advantage. The problem is that very few people are consciously aware of what this process is and how it can be applied.

Do you know what your most important resource and capability are and how to use them to your best advantage? If your answer to this vital question is no, then you should find this book on the Planagement System of enormous value to you and your future.

2

The Unbelievable Cost

IT IS DIFFICULT for individuals and organizations to accurately measure the precise cost of managing momentum with obsolete practices.

The Cost to Individuals

For the individual, the cost is a life lived well below his inherent potential. To waste time is to waste life, and there is no way known to recapture lost time. Yet people do not use their time to their best advantage. How can they when they lack direction and therefore a purpose to build toward one day at a time? If someone lacks a system for doing more, in less time, with better results, he is bound to waste a lot of time, which, in turn, results in an average or below-average life.

The Cost to Management

Surveys have indicated that United States business is losing over $400 million each day because of obsolete work methods and management practices. Researchers have estimated that the efficiency rate in most offices is less than 60 percent. And remember, efficiency is only *doing things right*. Effectiveness is *doing the right things*.

Many leading business authorities feel that we are not doing the right things and that 80 percent of today's management practices may be obsolete. Based on these two factors, the loss per day probably exceeds $2 billion.

It is a popular fallacy that computers, high-speed copying machines, and advanced office systems have increased office productivity. On the whole, this is not the case, because these devices have merely increased the *volume* of information. They have not increased the value of the data or the real productivity of the worker, nor have they reduced the number of workers processing the data.

While managers are prone to point to workers' productivity as the prime area for increased efficiency, the poor productivity factor most often mentioned by executives participating in a survey conducted by the American Management Associations * was "lack of well-defined organizational or departmental goals and objectives." And that's a management failure.

Sixty-three percent of the respondents said executive productivity was a "serious concern" in the operation of business and industry today, and they generally agreed it was tied directly to achievement of goals and profits. The most frequent complaints were that executives become too bogged down in day-to-day operations to think and plan on a long-range basis, and that there is an absence of performance standards constructed by the manager, his superior, the people affected, and senior management. Additional managerial deficiencies cited included:

1. Working at cross-purposes with other managers.
2. Lack of understanding of the job of managing.
3. Failure to keep an operation in proper perspective with relation to its impact on total company performance.
4. Failure to consciously adopt a philosophy of management and carry through with it.
5. Failure to develop people—too many managers fear strength.

One of the primary conclusions of the survey was: "It is time to forget the grandiose notion that managers naturally manage properly. We executives—from middle managers to presidents—need all the help we can get." Still, few managers, and only a small percentage of companies, were making efforts to evaluate executive productivity.

* Herman S. Jacobs and Katherine Jillson, *Executive Productivity*. An AMA Survey Report. AMACOM, 1974.

The Cost to the United States

The cost of this lag in executive productivity is greater than the tremendous dollar losses already mentioned. The United States has about 6 percent of the world's population. Of this 6 percent, far less than 1 percent are engaged in meeting the responsibilities of managing a national output that accounts for over 40 percent of the world's total goods and services.

The high standard of living in this country is largely dependent on the capabilities and skills of the American manager, and if the great majority of our managers and management practices are obsolete, it is a danger to our future and our position relative to other nations. Some economic experts have projected that the United States may cease to be the leading industrial country before the end of this century.

Americans are steadily losing confidence in themselves, their companies, their government, and their future. If this hopelessness continues, the United States will join the list of declining nations. Historians have pointed out that our country may be a dying civilization and might soon join the civilizations that have perished before us. All great civilizations go through a life cycle, beginning with struggle and ending with decadence. When building a civilization, people have faith in a new order and the courage to take the actions necessary to bring about that order. At the summit of the civilization, the people enjoy liberty and material abundance. But this ripeness contains the seeds of decay. People became selfish, complacent, and eventually apathetic. They no longer believe in the ideals that once sustained them; they become passive and dependent and allow their once vital institutions to decline. The original builders of the civilization are superseded by bureaucrats, and liberty is crushed by tyrannical policies and procedures.

It is instructive to note that the average life span of past civilizations has been 200 years. Unhappily, it does not take a great deal of imagination to see in our own history the stages just described. Our 200th birthday will be reached in July 1976, and the Bicentennial is viewed with mixed emotions by Americans. Many are so apathetic that there is a very real concern that there will be insufficient enthusiasm to generate an appropriate celebration.

Perhaps more articles are being written than ever before in our history that put the United States in a very poor light. We seem to be experiencing some sort of morbid and obsessive self-criticism that if prolonged will erode all trust in our president, our government, and ourselves. Can it be that the wonderful dream that created the United States is dying? Is history repeating itself with our own great and beloved nation? What is your opinion—is the United States dying?

Those who answer yes to that question should ask themselves what can be done to reverse the trend and reestablish the strengths that made us a great nation, built on the most challenging and rewarding dreams that man has yet conceived.

I feel we can, and we will, reestablish ourselves. A resurgence is possible at any stage in the life cycle. Once we recognize the stage we are in, we can begin to generate a new and even greater cycle for our civilization   if we have the faith and courage to take the actions each of us will be required to take. Granted, it's a big challenge, but can we really afford to fail to meet it?

Perhaps we can find some inspiration and encouragement in Daniel H. Burnham's challenge: "Make no little plans; they have no magic to stir men's blood and probably themselves will not be realized. Make big plans; aim high in hope and work, remembering that a noble, logical diagram once recorded will never die, but long after we are gone will be a living thing, asserting itself with ever-growing insistency." *

* Quoted in *The Treasure Chest*, edited by Charles L. Wallis. New York: Harper & Row, 1965.

3

Human Hang-ups
That Must Be Overcome

THE SITUATION described in the first two chapters presents us with both a tremendous problem and an unlimited opportunity. The primary problem is psychological because it is basic human hang-ups that prevent the vast majority of people from living up to their potential. The Dutch have a wonderful old saying: "If everybody would sweep his own front porch, the whole city would be clean." We must take a broom to our personal porches if we are to make the progress we are capable of and capitalize on our enormous opportunities. If we can master our human hang-ups, we will begin to achieve much more success.

Man's Thinking Machine

First and foremost, we must establish a better understanding of ourselves and our major capabilities. Man's most important capability is his ability to think. Everyone has been blessed with a mind—his own personal thinking machine—but since very few people understand how their thinking machines work, they don't know how to operate them effectively. Ask yourself the question, "What are the steps my mind goes through to make a good decision?" Do you know the clear answer to this question? Probably not. Most people don't and therefore lack a checklist for making better decisions faster.

When an employee presents an idea or a program, he is often told, "It isn't good enough—go back and think about it some more." Suppose you said this to someone and he replied, "All right, but please tell me how to think about it. What are the steps I need to go through to think?" How would you answer him? Chances are you couldn't, and yet the ability to think well and make sound, timely decisions frequently determines who will succeed and who will fail.

Three Common Dislikes

Generally speaking, people don't like what they don't understand, and since they don't understand how to think, they don't like to think. Some psychologists have concluded that there are three things people don't like to do: they don't like to think, they don't like to use orderly procedures, and they don't like paperwork. Assuming these psychologists are correct and common observation supports their conclusion then the average person has three very serious dislikes to overcome if he is to progress and be successful.

Anyone who doesn't like to think will be reluctant to exercise his thinking machine and as a result will have a static or declining mind. His indecisions or poor decisions will confirm the tragic fact that he is using very little of his mind.

The dislike of orderly procedures is another costly human weakness. Research has clearly shown that "a systematic way of doing something is *always* more efficient and less time-consuming than a disorderly approach that may require doing the same thing over several times in order to get it right." *

Time is an unrecapturable resource. The amount of success people achieve is determined in large measure by how wisely they use their time. Since most people don't like to use orderly procedures, this lack of self-discipline costs them time and reduces the success they enjoy. There are a number of helpful books on time management, but unfortunately, few people take the time to read them. It seems to be a human failing to spend time chopping wood but never pause to sharpen the ax. Do you have a system for managing your time? What is the orderly procedure that anyone can use to do more in less time with better results?

Most people don't like paperwork. This, too, is a serious weakness because it forces them to depend on their listening skills and memories for information, and, on the average, we remember

* Charles H. Kepner and Benjamin B. Tregoe, *The Rational Manager*. New York: McGraw-Hill Book Company, 1965.

less than 10 percent of what we hear. It has been said that if we hear it, we will forget it; if we write it, we will remember it; and if we live it, we will understand it.

Scientists and educators have shown that people have a better chance of remembering and understanding information when several senses are enlisted in the learning experience. For example, if we apply only one of our senses—say, hearing—we will remember very little. But if we both hear and see something, we are much more likely to remember the essentials.

Writing requires us to use two senses: seeing and touch. Therefore when we write something, we probably think it out much more thoroughly than we would if we just talked about it. We often don't listen well to what we or anyone else says, but we almost always remember what we write down. And once we truly acquire and store a piece of knowledge, it is an available resource for the rest of our lives; we can draw on it to better understand situations and make sounder decisions. Your knowledge bank is one of your most important resources.

The Importance of Direction

Because people do not like to think, use orderly procedures, or do paperwork, they rarely apply these disciplines to establish a sound direction. And obviously, unless one knows where he is going, it will be difficult or impossible for him to get there.

The person who has no direction will probably lack the drive and motivation to accomplish very much. Because he does not have a motive (objective), he will not take action, and he will be perceived as a complacent, nonmotivated individual who is going nowhere, a ship without a rudder. Psychologists tell us that a person with no objective frequently sinks into a state of depression.

Organizations that lack direction also tend to sink. Only one new business out of ten will survive its first year. Of a hundred dreams translated into business ventures, only one will exist for ten years.

Why do so few dreams endure to become productive realities? To paraphrase T. S. Eliot, between the idea and the reality, a shadow falls. This shadow takes several forms, but perhaps the failure to establish a clear direction at the beginning of a new venture is the most significant.

Lack of direction contributes to the demise of organizations just as it does to the demise of individuals because it signifies a lack of belief. William James emphasized the importance of commitment when he said: "Our belief at the beginning of a doubtful undertaking is the one thing that insures the successful outcome of our venture." We can easily distinguish between the committed individual and one who is passing through, testing an idea rather than living it, and we decide whom to support accordingly. Commitment is a key factor in success.

The Necessity for Discipline

Another form of the shadow between the idea and its realization is lack of discipline. How often have you known a person with great ideas whose freedom of mind was not supported by the discipline to activate those ideas? "Oh, he talks a good game, but he never really gets things done" is a saying we have all heard, perhaps even about ourselves. There is no point in being dedicated to an idea if you don't do everything to insure its success. The failure of new businesses is usually due to a lack of willingness and/or know-how to plan, manage, and control them.

Since it is human nature to resist self-discipline, many people resign themselves to living in the shadow of their own potential. A few entrepreneurs, however, have committed themselves to a disciplined effort to make their ideas a reality, believing that it is better to fail trying to accomplish something important than to be successful in nothing at all. They recognize that in order to lift the "shadow," one must risk failure. The distinguishing characteristic of an entrepreneur is his willingness to take risks in order to make an idea happen. He knows that the most satisfying part of a journey is not the destination, but the journey itself.

Managing Change

Change is one more form of the shadow between the idea and its accomplishment. Often we get a good idea only to see it destroyed by some factor we did not anticipate. Since we live in an age of constant change, we must learn to manage change to our advantage. We must develop a skill for consistently managing inconsistent situations in a way that produces gain. To do this, we need to establish a standard by which to monitor, measure, and influence change.

Individuals and organizations that do not learn to master change will allow change to determine their future. They will not obtain the benefits described by William Ellery Channing in "the Free Mind":

I call that mind free which is not passively framed by outward circumstances, which is not swept away by the torrent of events, which is not the creature of accidental impulse, but which bends events to its own improvement, and acts from an inward spring, from immutable principles which it has deliberately espoused.*

Other Hang-ups

Among the other common hang-ups people face in trying to live up to their potential is the human propensity for establishing a habit. We become so comfortable with a routine that we substitute the management of momentum for the thinking required to manage the potential. This common approach to things does not challenge our minds and often results in a mediocre existence.

People also have a tendency to make the simple complex, and the complex difficult or impossible. The English language is a good example of this inclination. The 500 most commonly used words in English have over 14,000 definitions among them. We frequently use words that do not have a precise definition, or at least one that is commonly understood. Some illustrations are "planning," "growth," "thinking," and "strategy." It is easier for us to resort to these nebulous terms than to carefully choose more exact words that leave no doubt as to what we mean. This lazy approach is a roadblock to understanding and communicating. Differences in education, experience, and frames of reference add to the problem.

Procrastination is the flab of an undisciplined mind. This common hang-up prevents us from making our ideas happen when we want them to. The problem is compounded by a tendency to skip or forget what we find difficult or troublesome.

Unfortunately, some people regard questions as a sign of stupidity or inexperience. But it is the questions we ask of others and of ourselves that stimulate thought. A questioning mind is a healthy, open, growing mind. In the rush to a final or perfect answer, we often turn off our thinking machine too quickly and eventually it stagnates. Obsolete people are anxious talkers with quick answers, rather than skilled listeners who know the right questions to ask in a logical sequence.

Another hang-up is an imbalance between logic and emotion. These two faculties are frequently viewed on an either/or basis, rather than as a natural combination. In every meeting between peo-

* Quoted in *The Treasure Chest*, edited by Charles L. Wallis. New York: Harper & Row, 1965.

ple, both facts and feeling are present, but instead of being communicated, they are assumed to be picked up. People are startled when someone asks them: "Do you know this to be true, and if so, why?" or "If you are guessing, what is the basis of your guess?" This kind of question is often the beginning of conscious and communicated thought, with improved understanding as the result.

The Value of a System

In order to overcome human hang-ups we must gain a better understanding of how our minds work. A systematic approach based on the establishment of sound direction should enable us to more rapidly identify, gather, organize, analyze, and present the minimum amount of information we require to make better decisions faster.

Though it is the conquest of outer space that captures man's imagination, what we need most is mastery of inner space. Mortimer J. Adler recognized our important opportunity to pioneer this new frontier:

> We often think of ourselves as living in a world which no longer has any unexplored frontiers. We speak of pioneering as a thing of the past. But in doing so, we forget that the greatest adventure of all still challenges us—what Mr. Justice Holmes called "the adventure of the human mind." Men may be hemmed in geographically, but every generation stands on the frontiers of the mind. In the world of ideas, there is always pioneering to be done, and it can be done by anyone who will use the equipment with which he is endowed. The great ideas belong to everyone.*

The Planagement System is based on the workings of the human mind. It provides the tools the individual needs to consciously use his mind to better plan, manage, and control himself, his present situation (including his job), and his future. It is important to realize that the Planagement System is just a tool, and as such depends on its user. Compare this tool to a hammer: A hammer can build a building or break a window, create a work of art or destroy a human life—the difference depends on the intent, the skill, and the discipline of its user. In order to be effective, the Planagement System requires a user who has the self-discipline to build on his greatest strengths and overcome his hang-ups.

* From an article in *The Saturday Review.* Cited in *The Treasure Chest,* edited by Charles L. Wallis. New York: Harper & Row, 1965.

4

The Unlimited Opportunity

In ORDER to build a tool that will assist individuals and organizations to capitalize on their unlimited opportunity and overcome their major problems, it is necessary to establish the criteria or product specifications the tool must meet. This is the approach that was taken in developing the Planagement System. The first step was to become aware of the existing management situation. This meant identifying the primary problems, opportunities, strengths, weaknesses, potentials, and (perhaps most important) basic needs. The needs were listed under three categories: individual, manager, and organization. Then a profile of the needed system was evolved, and the concepts, techniques, and tools required to establish it were developed, together with the criteria the system was to meet or exceed. The most important needs that were identified, and the criteria used to measure results, are listed in Tables 1, 2, and 3. Several others were identified, but they could all be included under one or more of the 17 primary needs listed in the tables.

These needs and criteria for measuring results presented a tremendous challenge and a great opportunity. I am certain the Planagement System has met the challenge, but it is difficult to convince someone of the system's chances for success unless he is willing to apply it and measure its results himself. *This is exactly what you are requested to do as you read this book.* You are asked to apply the Plan-

Table 1. Major individual needs and criteria used to measure results.

INDIVIDUAL NEEDS	CRITERIA
1. To understand and better apply the logic and common-sense processes.	1. An increased ability to make better decisions faster; a system for gathering, processing, using, storing, managing, and controlling information.
2. To establish a sound direction and to convert developed ideas into reality.	2. A sound, written plan including objectives and the scheduled actions required to accomplish the objectives within an established time frame.
3. To use time more wisely.	3. An orderly, systematic approach to situations supported by a system to do more in less time with better results.
4. To better anticipate and manage change to measurable advantage.	4. A standard that reduces the impact of change and contributes to the consistent management of inconsistent situations in a way that produces constant gain.
5. To overcome human hang-ups and develop the needed self-discipline to identify and achieve potential.	5. Continuous and improving use of the Planagement System; measurably expanding gain from the activity.
6. To improve self-image and increase confidence.	6. An expanding positive plan that is acted on by a growing person.

agement System to your own situation, and then measure the results in your own life and in your organization against the challenging Planagement criteria.

Planning and Management—One Job

During the development phase of the Planagement System, several key factors that had a significant influence on the structuring of the system emerged. One was that planning and management were commonly viewed and practiced as separate functions. This belief was often supported by separating responsibilities into planning and doing types of jobs. People were thought of as being planners, not doers, or as doers, not planners. Several organizations I have worked with had established a separate planning job apart from operations. The person who held this job was supposed to develop

Table 2. Major manager needs and criteria used to measure results.

MANAGER NEEDS	CRITERIA
1. To understand the management function and what elements comprise an excellent or ideal manager; to master the job of a manager.	1. A definition of manager and the management function; a system that assists the manager to better meet his responsibilities; a profile of the ideal manager.
2. To avoid becoming obsolete and being passed over for advancement; to learn to live more comfortably with change and to manage it to advantage.	2. A living plan for the manager's area of responsibility, including a formal self-development program that allows him to perform better in his present job while preparing for the responsibilities, challenges, recognition, and compensation of the next job.
3. To enjoy work.	3. A guideline for compiling descriptions of jobs that managers would enjoy doing.
4. To simplify the management job.	4. One program that integrates many fragmented management programs and that is easy to teach and apply.
5. To make better decisions faster and to make the decisions happen.	5. A manual management information system that quickly identifies, gathers, organizes, analyzes, and presents the minimum amount of information required to make a sound decision and to help make that decision happen.

good plans because of his planning knowledge and skills, and the operating or line managers were supposed to implement the plans.

This view of planning and management is neither conceptually sound nor operationally practical. When planning was attempted in this manner, the plan frequently was not implemented. After the failure became apparent, it was very difficult to pinpoint responsibility or take corrective action because the operating people blamed the plan and the planner, while the planner insisted that the failure was due to poor implementation. Understanding and resolving this constant conflict between planning and management required going back to the basics and asking, What is management? What are the primary functions of a manager?

Table 3. Major organization needs and criteria used to measure results.

ORGANIZATION NEEDS	CRITERIA
1. To establish a purpose or mission; to identify and achieve potential; to set sound objectives that will result in continuous profit, growth, and satisfaction by the organization's people and publics.	1. A clearly written plan that includes all these needs; consistent maintenance of an optimum balance between these needs.
2. To create a positive climate within the organization so that the needed resources will be attracted to the organization and will stay with it so that its expanding plan will be constantly supported by the required resources.	2. A system that identifies, develops, and places the right person in the right job; an organizational climate that balances individual freedom with the discipline necessary to assure organization direction.
3. To contribute to the development of all employees in order to increase their productivity and desire to support the organization and its objectives.	3. A single, teachable system of management that integrates a number of management concepts and fragmented programs and promotes the self-development of all employees so that they want to identify, manage, and achieve their own potential.
4. To be better able to anticipate, adapt, manage, and influence change to advantage.	4. A living plan kept current through exception reporting, with the desired results being achieved through the use of key operating ratios.
5. To establish a management information system that enables management to make better decisions faster.	5. A total management system that can be used by all managers to individually or collectively identify, gather, organize, analyze, and present the minimum information required to continuously make sound, timely decisions and to make those decisions happen according to plan.
6. To effectively and efficiently convert sound concepts into reality.	6. A practical method for converting sound concepts into reality.

There was general agreement that the basic functions inherent in the management responsibility are: planning, organizing, implementing (includes communication, coordination, and motivation), controlling, and updating (keeping current). In analyzing these basic functions, it became apparent that planning, organizing, controlling, and updating—four of the five functions (80 percent)—were really planning in nature, while only one of the five (20 percent) was a doing function. This observation led to the conclusion that planning and management were essentially the same function because most of the manager's skills and time were devoted to planning, not doing. This insight contributed to creating the proprietary trade name Planagement, ® and helped us to establish an integrated planning/management function to replace the usual nebulous procedure.

Criteria Used to Develop Planagement

When asked the definition of planning, managers could rarely answer. Because they had no clear definition of the planning function, they held many mistaken beliefs about planning. Some of these mistaken beliefs were:

Planning is a separate function from operations.
A planner and a doer are two different people.
Planning creates more paperwork.
Short- and long-range plans are separate.
Planning is new, complicated, and no fun.
Creativity is threatened by planning.
Because of rapid change, you can no longer plan effectively.
Planning should be done only at the top level of management.
A perfect plan is possible.
Once the plan is established, you do not change it; therefore a plan is static.
Planning cannot be delegated.
Everyone understands and believes in planning.

These twelve mistaken beliefs, along with some others, contributed to an approach that virtually assured poor planning for both the organization and the individual.

Just how important is planning? One survey, covering companies that earned more than 10 percent after-tax return on their investment, disclosed that the only common denominator was that top managers spent more than 50 percent of their time on planning. It is generally estimated that at least 70 percent of a company's future success depends on the soundness of its strategy—which is identified through the application of a planning discipline.

Few companies have been able to develop a successful planning program, though many very skillful managers have tried to because they recognize the importance of a sound planning approach.

Why do planning programs so frequently fail? Some of the predominant reasons are:

1. Lack of understanding of the planning process itself. If the planning process is not clearly understood, then it will be difficult or impossible to apply it in a formal or consistent manner. Many times the planning process will start with the establishment of an objective (forecast), which is the fifth step, not the first, of a sound planning process. In addition, the mechanics of planning (the science) are incomplete and often are not blended with the human side of planning (the art), resulting in an incomplete, misunderstood, or confused picture of what planning is and how it works. When the planning process is not understood, planning tends either to be so flexible that there is little or no direction, or so rigid that there is an overemphasis on plans that may be obsolete and underemphasis on the continuous, dynamic *process* that helps to anticipate and successfully manage change.

2. A second contributor to poor planning is the lack of a plan that will identify and establish a method for planning (based on an understanding of the planning process) and a program for implementing the plan at all management levels. The plan for planning should be written and a feedback system should be created to measure its soundness, how well it is being implemented, and what results are being generated from its application.

3. The first two reasons for planning failures normally contribute to the third reason, which is frequently fatal for a planning program—lack of understanding, support, participation, enthusiasm, and urgency on the part of top management for the planning effort. There may be much talk about planning, but little will be done about it if key management figures do not set the example or provide the needed guidelines and direction. The entire organization will not be planning conscious and individual employees will not develop the self-discipline that sound planning requires.

4. Two closely related errors in planning are centralization of the effort and separating it from operations. Also, if long-range and short-range planning are not integrated, the results are confusion and additional steps. If planning is not made a part of every manager's responsibility, the chances of its working are greatly reduced,

as are its benefits. Since a manager's job is to plan, organize, implement, control, and update, and four out of five of these management functions are planning in nature, planning is a major part of every manager's job. If you separate the planner from the doer, then whenever something goes wrong, the doer will blame the plan and the planner will claim the failure was in the implementation. This argument is very difficult to resolve.

5. The lack of a systematic approach to the planning function often results in a fragmented program with a duplication of effort and some serious areas of conflict. Planning should be an integrated program that combines planning/management/communication/coordination/motivation/development (of individual and organization)/control/and compensation based on results. A basic requirement for maximum profits and growth is to have the right person, in the right job, at the right cost, at the right time—and an integrated planning program should assist in doing this.

6. Sound planning cannot be forced on an organization; it must become part of the whole management process and should be tailored to the organization and the requirements of its managers. The approach is one of selling people on the idea through a program of education, emphasizing the self-development aspects of applying the planning process. To do the proper job of education requires both patience and time, and if either are insufficient, then the planning program will suffer.

7. Once a plan is generated, it must be reviewed and a continuous feedback system must be created to keep it current. Otherwise the planning process will degenerate into a once-a-year exercise that fails because of lack of attention. It is very discouraging to develop a plan and have it ignored. This usually happens just once. Then the planner assumes his efforts are unwanted or impractical.

These seven contributors to poor planning are not, of course, a complete list, but they are useful in establishing positive criteria for a planning program. Some of these positive criteria are:

1. The planning system should be simple and practical.

2. It should be selective in nature to avoid a dollar's worth of planning for a dime's worth of results (or a dime's worth of planning for a dollar's worth of results).

3. The system should be universally applicable, with a common format and method that managers at all levels can easily learn and apply individually and collectively.

4. The planning/management system should be firm enough

to provide direction, and at the same time flexible enough to anticipate and manage change to advantage.

5. The system should provide the essential elements of information in a precise way so that better decisions can be made more rapidly.

6. A living plan that will consistently deal with changes and problems through a constant feedback system based on exception reporting should be written.

7. The system should be designed so that it stimulates management commitment and support.

8. Paperwork should be minimized, communications improved, and information handling simplified.

9. The system should contribute to integrating individual objectives and development with organization objectives and development.

10. The system should measurably assist in the development of the individual.

11. The system should provide objective standards for measuring performance and appropriately rewarding it.

12. A common format should be provided so that individual and job plans can be communicated, coordinated, and consolidated into team plans, functional plans, and product plans; and so that program and project plans can be consolidated into plans for a division or the entire organization.

13. The planning/management system should stimulate creativity through a sound balance of freedom and discipline. That is, the organizational climate should allow people enough freedom to create their own plans for their own areas of responsibility yet should simultaneously provide a framework of established organization direction and discipline.

14. Sound objectives should be developed and established through use of the system. The integrity and soundness of the plan should be objectively established by its creator and approver.

15. The planning system should integrate many fragmented programs into one simple, easily understood and practiced system.

16. The system should be effective in identifying the *right things to do* and efficient in assisting people to *do things right.*

17. The planning/management method should blend scientific management with the behavioral sciences.

18. The system should be evolved from the application of common sense, economic sense, and sound, professional principles.

These 18 positive criteria, combined with the 17 primary needs and criteria for measuring results listed in Tables 1–3, were used to establish the program specifications the Planagement System was required to meet or exceed.

Since the Planagement System was designed to overcome basic human hang-ups, it could not be a specific set of rules, a series of procedures, a set style of managing, an answer in itself, or a substitute for thinking and managing. It had to be based on thinking and managing, and in that sequence. It had to devise a total management and information system that would provide the minimum amount of information required to make sound decisions fast. In addition, in order to meet or exceed the established criteria, the system had to spark the unrealized potential, creative ability, and entrepreneurial spirit that lie dormant in almost everyone. The theory was that once individual employees were growing, the organization itself would develop and grow.

A Sense of Mission

The key to growth is a planning/management system that provides a proper purpose or mission. This mission is the leading edge of sound planning and should be carefully conceived.

Do you have a personal mission? Does your organization have a mission? You might be tempted to answer: "No, do we need one? Why?"

Because "mission" is a highly charged word with connotations of sacrifice and idealism, it frequently evokes a negative or embarrassed response—"Let's quit talking and get back to work and make a buck." But a sense of mission has often been vitally important in increasing a company's profit and growth, as well as the personal job satisfaction of its employees. Today it is even more important to establish a company meaning or mission as a sort of touchstone of continuity in an age of rapid change.

It is just as important to know why a company exists as it is to know what a company does. Many company officers will quickly answer that their company exists to make money, that this is its only purpose. While profit may be a prime purpose, a company's mission is usually far more than just making money. Great companies such as International Business Machines, International Harvester Company, and the Bovaird Supply Company have defined their missions and converted them into operating practices that have measurably contributed to their spirit and success.

Some missions are very simple statements such as: "This company is committed to maximizing growth and profits through the growth and development of its employees." This type of mission may be turned into action by establishing a goal that in five years at least *x* percent of the company's volume and profit will come from sources not presently in being, and these new opportunities will be managed by people promoted from within. Another example of a statement of mission is: "To stimulate healthy growth, pay reasonable dividends, create opportunities for employees, and provide job security through the profits and growth of the company."

Separate missions may be established for the company's various publics:

Stockholders: To provide the optimum investment opportunity, tailored to the needs of the stockholders, without sacrificing the needs of the company.

Employees: To provide the maximum opportunity for growth and development together with a climate that is challenging, secure, fun, and rewarding.

Customers: To provide quality products and services at a fair price.

Suppliers: To deal always in a manner that will gain their respect and favored support.

Served markets: To actively participate in the industries served in order to insure their soundness, vitality, and growth.

Community: To actively support the communities in which the company operates so that they may offer attractive services and opportunities to employees and visitors.

Government: To influence government to give constructive support to the company, the company's publics, and the company's served markets in particular, and private enterprise in general.

Some companies have as their prime purpose the establishment of a leadership position in the markets served. This type of mission is typically converted to a strategy of market dominance as measured by the percent of market penetration.

Organizations sometimes change or supplement their missions to reflect an altered situation. Recently, one company found itself in serious economic difficulty. Top management supplemented its statement of mission with the priority goal "survival of the firm," and all strategic and operating decisions and policies reflected this emphasis. Everybody in that company knew the name of the current game and could act supportively. This was quite a change for a company that had had as its previous mission a commitment to growth, with a strategy of increasing the assets employed in the enterprise.

A good example of the contribution a statement of mission can make toward managing change was in the ill-fated moonshot when the oxygen tank exploded as the astronauts approached their moon landing. The original mission was to land the astronauts on the moon so they could accomplish certain tasks. Detailed schedules had been established. Then the malfunction happened, and the immediate response was to invoke the mission of bringing the men home safely. All other objectives were abandoned in favor of that vital mission.

Company missions are established for the following major reasons:

1. To provide productive direction.
2. To provide the belief that will create an organization climate that inspires people to achieve excellence and satisfaction in their jobs (maximum motivation).
3. To provide a needed discipline to make the right kind of things happen.
4. To communicate the company's reasons for existence.
5. To create a basis for measuring success in terms other than profit.

One of the primary definitions of mission in *Webster's* is: "Task assigned, an act of sending a body of persons to perform a service or carry on an activity" This dictionary definition comes fairly close to delineating the purpose of an organization. If the organization is a profit-making enterprise, then its profitability—"continuing gain from the activity"—requires a commitment to something more than what presently exists. If there is nothing to strive for, no ideal, then little gain will be achieved. The organization will merely manage its momentum, not its potential, and this posture will determine the organization's performance in economic terms.

The Planagement System's mission is to build on the most important strengths of the individual and the organization, while identifying and capitalizing on their greatest unrealized potential. It contributes to achieving this potential by applying a consistent method for establishing sound objectives and a systematic action-oriented approach toward managing change to advantage and doing more, in less time, with better results.

Part II

The Concept

5

The Greatest
Unrealized Potential

*I find the great thing in this world is not so much where we
stand as in what direction we are moving.*
—OLIVER WENDELL HOLMES

*Hell begins on the day when God grants us a clear vision of all that we might
have achieved, of all the gifts which we have wasted, of all that we might
have done which we did not do.*

—GIAN-CARLO MENOTTI

*There is a tide in the affairs of men
Which, taken at the flood, leads on to fortune;
Omitted, all the voyage of their life,
Is bound in shallows and in miseries.*
—WILLIAM SHAKESPEARE

YOU ARE URGED to consider the above thoughts carefully as you read
this chapter because you are probably using only a very small part of
your greatest potential. As we said earlier, most individuals and organizations are achieving less than 15 percent of their potential.

In the preceding chapters you have been asked where this potential lies. Most managers recognize that their greatest potential is
in their people, but that is where they stop. When asked *where* in
their people, very few have been able to answer. As individuals and
as managers, we need to know where this potential exists so we may
tap it.

The Human Brain

The greatest human potential is in the mind. How does the mind work? What are the steps that the human brain goes through to make a decision, generate an idea, solve a problem? People who cannot answer these questions—who do not understand how their minds work—are probably not using their minds to best advantage.

Research has indicated that the average human being uses only about 5 percent of his brain. Managers, because of the various disciplines they have to employ, are reported to use somewhere between 10 and 13 percent of their brains. Einstein, one of our greatest thinkers, used only about 22 percent of his brain. How do scientists know that we use such a small percentage of our brain? What is the basis of their research?

The average human brain weighs between three and four pounds and is smaller than 100 cubic inches. It can store an estimated 2,000,000,000,000,000 bits of information—more than 20,000 times the quantity of information contained in the entire set of the *Encyclopaedia Britannica.* Put in other terms, to duplicate with present technology the capacity of one human brain would require a computer larger than the earth itself.

Some scientists have concluded from human brains willed for study that the brain cells we exercise are a different color than those we do not exercise—just as the white meat in a chicken (wings and breast) is the unexercised meat and the dark meat (legs and second joints) is the exercised meat. On this basis, they have estimated that the average person exercises only about 5 percent of his brain, managers 10 to 13 percent, and Einstein some 22 percent.

You may question these research conclusions; however, their absolute accuracy is of secondary importance. The fact is that most people believe they are living well below their true potential, that they are not doing nearly as well as they are capable of doing.

Common Sense

How do you tap this potential? Primarily through understanding how your mind works and acquiring self-discipline to overcome the human hang-ups described in Chapter 3. It is of vital importance to understand the sense that is common to every human being, for unless we do, we will not consciously work our minds to advantage.

What is common sense? We often refer to it but can seldom articulate its specific meaning. One definition of common sense is "sound, ordinary sense; good judgment." When we look up the word *sense,* we find it defined as "the ability to reach intelligent conclusions." Combining the two definitions, we might say: "Common sense implies a capacity for making practical and reasonable decisions."

Our definition of common sense leads to a consideration of man's thinking machine, that fantastic resource that allows us to make decisions. The soundness of our decisions depends on many factors, but none is more important than a thorough knowledge of how our minds work. With this knowledge we will be able to increase the 5 percent utilization that research tells us is average.

The Logic Process

The thinking process of the healthy, disciplined mind is known as the logic process. Once you learn how to use this process systematically—so that it becomes almost second nature—you will begin to work smarter, not just harder. You will start to make better decisions faster. You will more often identify and do the right things, in addition to doing more things right and more rapidly. The key elements (in sequence) that comprise the logic process are:

1. Define the situation.
2. Analyze the situation.
3. Develop alternatives.
4. Decide on the best alternative.
5. Take action to make the decision happen.
6. Justify the decision (know the reason why).
7. Redefine the situation as change requires.

This process is constantly repeated, and often works so fast that we are not even conscious of it. The danger, of course, is that it may become so automatic that we skip steps without realizing it—which is why this checklist is so valuable for sound decision making.

Since the logic process is universally applicable, it allows you to understand and manage a situation without having had extensive personal experience with that situation. This is the process that a doctor uses in diagnosis. He defines the situation by asking a patient, "How do you feel?" or "Where does it hurt?" Then he analyzes the situation, using the information the patient gives him and his own observations. After considering various alternative treatments and medicines, he decides what action is required to cure the disease. Finally, he may justify the diagnosis by consulting other doctors, and change the treatment according to how the patient is progressing (redefine the situation). Essentially the same approach is used by a lawyer handling a case and an engineer dealing with an opportunity or problem.

Even though the logic process (the decision-making or problem-solving process) is an innate human faculty, we sometimes ignore, casually skip, or forget some of the steps that comprise the process. These mental lapses can be very costly. The biggest danger of all, however, is in not learning how to use our minds to begin with, in failing to develop this innate faculty, because then we will move only with momentum and resist situations that are different from what we are used to or comfortable with.

The progress we make, or don't make, is directly related to how well we use our heads. If we spend our lives doing things over instead of doing them right in the first place, then our lives will not be nearly as productive as they should be. If we fail to effectively apply lessons already learned to a constantly changing situation, then we will not learn from our mistakes, but will repeat them. Instead of offering us a beneficial challenge, change will frustrate and disappoint us.

Lack of direction is the root of indecision and hopelessness. A human being cannot live in a condition of emptiness for very long; if he is not growing toward something, he does not merely stagnate, he deteriorates—and becomes either depressed or destructive. Perhaps this is the explanation for the current drug problem, the violence, and even the phenomenon of the corporate dropout (the man who was born in 1920, died in 1965, and won't be buried until 1985). His "premature death" may be attributed to a lack of challenge on the job and boredom with life in general. The reason he finds himself in this sad situation is that he has not used his mind to establish direction—if he has any direction at all, it is as limited as the average TV screen.

Though thus far the situations described and the examples used have been virtually all negative, the overview is positive and exciting. The fact that you may use only 5 percent of your mind's potential should encourage you because the untapped resource is enormous. Once you understand how your thinking machine works, once you consciously grasp the significance of the logic process, you will become a problem preventer instead of a problem solver, a good listener instead of an anxious talker. By thinking first, then deciding, and then taking action, you will produce much better results than by automatically taking the action you are accustomed to.

The Sixth Sense

There is little question that the logic process and the capability of the brain are fundamental to common sense. But as important as the brain is, it is not the only factor. Common sense also employs the heart—the ability to empathize, feel, listen with genuine interest, trust the other person, and understand what is in his mind and heart.

True common sense is the product of a sound balance between logic and emotion. We quickly recognize and respect people who have a "sixth sense," an insight into those with whom they work and situations with which they deal. Perhaps it is this sixth sense that makes the difference between intelligence and wisdom. It does seem that people with common sense not only acquire knowledge but are also aware that the value of knowledge depends on how it is used. It is not just what they know; it is what they do with what they know and for what purpose.

One of the signs of a developed common sense is the willingness to constantly search with an open and inquiring mind for a better answer. Since this answer frequently lies in the wisdom, direction, and perspective of other people, common sense encompasses the social sciences.

There are a number of additional considerations, but if you consciously and consistently combine the logic process with your sixth sense, you should make considerable progress in developing your common sense and bridging the gap between your potential and your achievement.

Management by Objectives

As we have seen, it is not the objective or the plan of action that is the most crucial element, but rather the process that the mind goes through to establish a sound direction. We have also noted that many people and organizations do not understand this, and hence begin their planning programs with the objectives or the problem or the decision—which is the fourth step in the logic process—rather than with the first step, which is to define the situation. Because they do not go through the first three steps, the decision they make may be unsound.

This is a major reason why management by objectives can be dangerous. It is not my purpose here to take issue with the popular management-by-objectives concept. It has considerable merit, though the benefits that should be obtained are frequently reduced or lost because of unsound objectives and poor implementation. Many managers are now of the opinion that management by objectives is a complex procedure that can lead you in the wrong direction with a higher degree of assurance. Some (including myself) believe that we do not really manage by objectives, but rather by facts, judgment, and actions which establish the objectives.

The validity of the management-by-objectives concept depends on the assumption that an objective is sound in the first place. If *unsound* objectives are established, they will be accomplished to the detriment of the organization. Perhaps, then, we manage more by our assumptions than we do by the objectives we established.

Unfortunately, some managers are so myopic that they insist on accomplishing their established objectives no matter what the results are. They will rigidly hold to their original goals whether they are good or bad, right or wrong, still valid or no longer relevant. Some of the most common errors in management-by-objectives programs are:

1. The objectives established do not meet one or more of the following criteria for a sound objective:

Measurable: Does the objective clearly state *what* will happen *when?*

Feasible: Is the objective *practical;* can it be done?

Valuable: Is the *gain* (result) worth the effort?

Flexible: Can the objective *accommodate change,* and at the same time *provide direction?*

Suitable: Does it *support* the organization's and the supervisors' guidelines?

Achievable: Can it be *accomplished* through your efforts?

Acceptable: Will the needed *resources* be provided?

Commitment: Does the objective provide a *challenge* and arouse people's *interest?* Does it answer the question "What's in it for me?"

2. The thinking, facts, judgments, and assumptions from which the objectives are evolved and the actions required to make the objectives happen, are not documented and communicated; con-

sequently, there is little or no basis to measure soundness or manage change.

3. The individual is not given the opportunity to establish objectives for his or her area of responsibility. In this case, the process of management by objectives becomes impersonal and dictatorial because personal objectives are not united with organizational objectives.

4. Proper guidelines are not provided by the organization or the supervisor. Working without guidance can be compared to trying to solve a jigsaw puzzle without the picture of what the pieces add up to. Supporting effort will suffer, and supporting objectives will often miss the mark.

5. A method to measure progress in accomplishing the objectives is not devised. Without a monitoring system, the objectives may be forgotten or become out of date. Instead of a living goal, the objectives become the excuse for continuous activity, which may not accomplish results (or the right results). If there is no feedback system, people will feel the program is just another company project that got started but didn't go anywhere or accomplish anything important.

6. The objectives set for people do not relate to their jobs, and therefore never become a basis for measuring performance. Neither are they tied in with a salary incentive program. If there are no identified standards of performance, employees will feel confused and frustrated.

7. There is no priority of objectives; hence there are difficulties in communication, coordination, and consolidation of individual objectives with division and organization objectives. The result may be an overload that makes the objectives unachievable within the established time frame. When this happens, there is often disappointment with the program to the point where it may be dropped in favor of the previous, more comfortable, "informal" way of doing things.

8. The objectives set emphasize activity more than results. Unless the anticipated results of the program are clear to everyone, the program may not be continued because it requires a self-discipline that people usually want to avoid—at least at the beginning. Also, some people prefer not to be measured, either because of a lack of self-confidence or a fear that the program is being used.more as a club than as a constructive and supportive tool.

9. No formal method for coordinating and consolidating objectives is established. If the basic objectives are not identified, a

team will not be able to work on them collectively and thus avoid duplication or fragmentation. Though each person is accountable for his own objectives, he will sometimes have to assume support from another person, function, or division over which he has no control. This is where organization structure and practices often act as a blockade rather than a helpful channel. The situation can be remedied through the use of a formal communication/coordination tool which reflects an organization philosophy that "management means getting things done through other people *regardless of reporting relationships.*"

10. Misunderstanding of the basic concept and the benefits to be derived frequently contributes to the demise of management-by-objective programs. Unless the concept is clearly grasped, it will be difficult to establish an appropriate program for successful implementation.

Management by Logic

The essential thing to understand is that it is the process of the mind that establishes sound direction, and that prior to setting objectives we need first to define the situation, analyze the situation, and develop alternatives. In these first three steps we will begin to identify the potential in a situation and tap it. Then we will see a dramatic and measurable gain from our activity.

How can we objectively measure this gain? By comparing the historical and anticipated gains of the existing plan with the results of the new logical plan, using a basic common-sense approach to planning, management, and control.

Here is a typical example of the results that might be achieved in a profit-making organization if management uses logic. The company now has a sales volume of $1,000,000, total expenses of $800,000, and a profit plan of $200,000. Assume that the greatest unrealized potential is in the mind, and that managers are currently using only 10 percent of their mental capacity. By employing the logic process to develop a revised plan, the managers will be forced to exercise their minds and possibly use 11 instead of 10 percent of their mental capacity. This is bound to increase management effectiveness and efficiency.

The revised plan should evolve approximately as follows: Since management controls sales volumes and costs of sales, and since management effectiveness has increased by at least 10 percent (10 percent of the mind to 11 percent of the mind), then sales should also increase at least 10 percent and relative costs should decrease 10 percent. Thus the revised profit plan would show a sales volume of $1,100,000, total expenses of $720,000, and a revised profit plan of $380,000.

The gain can be clearly seen in a comparison of the two plans: In the revised plan, profit has increased by 90 percent ($180,000), and profit as a percentage of sales has risen from 20 percent to 34.5 percent. While admittedly this example is oversimplified, it does suggest how an existing plan and its results may be objectively compared to a plan based on the logic process and its results.

It was assumed in the example that the conscious application of the logic process by management would increase effectiveness. In numerous applications of the Planagement System to a wide variety of people, organizations, and situations, this assumption has proved valid—in fact, the gains have normally been underestimated.

It is this basic logic process that forms the foundation of the Planagement System, and it is through the conscious and continuous application of this process that the individual and the organization will be better able to identify and manage their greatest unrealized potential.

6

The Management of Potential

ONCE THE logic process is understood, a system can be evolved that integrates that process with the processes of planning, management, decision making, problem solving, creativity, development (for both individuals and organizations), communication, motivation, control, feedback, update, and management-of-change into one teachable process—Planagement. Planagement identifies an organization's potential, and through the creation of a healthy organizational climate that balances individual freedom with the discipline of organization direction, sparks the creative ability and the entrepreneurial spirit in people. This results in maximum motivation and productivity of employees. They will usually be enthusiastic about participating in the Planagement program because it answers their lurking question "What's in it for me?" They will begin to look upon their jobs as a business, and the company will provide more self-actualizing work. In addition, the company will develop a method for identifying and managing its potential, and so will the individual.

Introducing the Planagement System

It is important to introduce the Planagement program so that employees understand it and are receptive to participating in it. One of the best ways to accomplish this is to explain that the program is

44

based on how their own minds work, and that—because it integrates and simplifies many management concepts—it will make their jobs easier and their lives more productive.

The starting place would be to review the mind's logic process, as described in Chapter 5. Then the same process would be put in planning and management (Planagement) terminology. Once the Planagement process is understood, it would be related to the basic management process, which is to plan, organize, implement, control, and update. Next, it is important to clarify the planning process, which is nebulous in most minds. In considering the planning process in its simplest form, reflect for a moment on how you go about planning a *trip*. The normal sequence is:

Step 1. Establish *where* and *what* you are now (most overlook this vital and basic step and start with Step 2).
Step 2. Identify *where* you want to go.
Step 3. Define *how* you will get to where you want to go.
Step 4. Know *when* you expect to arrive.
Step 5. Establish *who* is going to do what.
Step 6. Confirm *how much* you are willing to pay.
Step 7. Know *why* you are making the trip.
Step 8. Continuously identify how you are doing, noting where you are now against your trip plan and incorporating changes as required to accomplish or enhance your plan.*

The overall Planagement Matrix is similar to this. It is shown in Table 4.

The Planagement approach to planning differs considerably from the way planning is normally done. To make its maximum contribution, Planagement requires a type of climate and communications that seldom exists in the typical organization. But if people and organizations commit themselves to the management of potential, they will not be reluctant to make basic changes, even though it is not easy or palatable to do so.

The individual will have to gain a better insight into his mind and personality. It is extremely difficult to be objective about self-analysis; however, the logical process does make introspection easier, and there are several psychological tools that can be of assistance in gaining better self-understanding.

* Copyright © 1974, Planagement, Inc.

Table 4. Planagement matrix.

STEPS	LOGIC PROCESS	PLANAGEMENT PROCESS	MANAGEMENT PROCESS	PLANNING PROCESS
1	Define the situation	Logic/facts/belief (science)	Plan	Where you are now; what you are now
2	Analyze the situation	Analysis/alternatives (science and art)	Plan	Where you are now; what you are now
3	Evolve alternatives	Judgments/assumptions/potentials (art)	Plan and organize	Where you are now; what you are now; where you want to go
4	Decide	Decision/objectives (direction)	Organize	Where you want to go
5	Take action	Plan of action (discipline)	Implement	How you will get there; when you expect to arrive; who is going to do what
6	Justify; know why	Why/justification (gain from the activity)	Control	How much you will pay; why you are going
7	Identify deviations	Control/exceptions/update/deviations/changes (living plan)	Control/update	How you are doing
The steps needed to make a decision and to make that decision a reality.	Process is repeated continuously. This is the process of the mind—the common-sense process.	Plan your work; work your plan; change your plan as change requires. Closed-loop systems approach.	Basic functions of professional management: to consistently manage inconsistent situations in such a way as to produce constant gain from the activity.	Basic steps of the planning process as related to planning a trip.

Setting the Right Climate

Introspection is also necessary for an organization that wishes to assess its own climate. The organization leader, through his management style and plans for the future, usually sets the organization's climate. But it is very difficult for him to evaluate his company's climate objectively since this is so close to being self-analysis. He may decide to use outsiders to determine it for him.

Industrial psychologists, professional managers, and management consultants have developed several methods for determining an organization's climate: attitude surveys, general questions on internal environment, and formal climate analysis surveys. Many other techniques are used, but these are the most common.

The climate of an organization needs to be carefully and constructively managed, for it determines what kind of human growth will be tolerated. And the profit and growth of an organization are directly dependent on the growth and development of its people. Climate has considerable influence on what kind of people will be attracted to the organization, as well as the degree to which people will flourish in the organization and whether they will *stay* in the organization. Individual productivity and creativity, and many other key elements, are also directly tied to the climate that exists.

Thus, one of the manager's biggest challenges is to create the type of climate where people will be motivated to do their best. No manager can really motivate his subordinates, as motivation has to come from within the individual, but the climate he creates will have a real impact on whether or not the people working for him want to do their best.

Management Styles

Two extreme styles of management—the now famous Theory X and Theory Y—are described in *The Human Side of Enterprise* * by Douglas McGregor. According to McGregor, the Theory X type of manager believes that:

- The average human being has an inherent dislike for work and will avoid it if he can.
- Because of this human characteristic of dislike for work, most people must be coerced, controlled, directed, and threatened with punishment to get them to put forth adequate effort toward the achievement of organizational objectives.

* New York: McGraw-Hill Book Company, 1960.

• The average human being prefers to be directed, wishes to avoid responsibility, has relatively little ambition, and wants security above all.

Obviously this type of manager creates a dictatorial climate with stringent controls. He insists that all planning and management be a one-man show. Under him, individual growth is limited, and the motivating techniques used could be characterized as "hire and fire" or "hold out a small carrot and carry a big stick."

In contrast, McGregor's Theory Y manager believes that:

• The expenditure of physical and mental effort in work is as natural as play or rest.
• External control and the threat of punishment are not the only means for bringing about effort toward organizational objectives. Man will exercise self-direction and self-control in the service of objectives to which he is committed.
• Commitment to objectives is a function of the rewards associated with their achievement.
• The average human being learns, under proper conditions, not only to accept but to seek responsibility.
• The capacity to exercise a relatively high degree of imagination, ingenuity, and creativity in the solution of organizational problems is widely, not narrowly, distributed in the population.
• Under the conditions of modern industrial life, the intellectual potentialities of the average human being are only partially utilized.

Under the Theory Y manager, the climate is considerably more positive than it is under the Theory X manager, simply because the boss believes in people and assumes they desire to grow and have the ability to do so. Robert Townsend * attributed his success at Avis Corporation primarily to the successful implementation of the Theory Y type of management, and McGregor has predicted that unless a manager successfully practices Theory Y, he, and his organization, probably will not be in existence by the end of the 1970s.

Perhaps the best test of the merits of Theory X versus those of Theory Y is to ask yourself which type of manager you would prefer to work for. Then imagine the climates generated by the X and Y styles and ask yourself which company you would want to join. Most people prefer the Theory Y approach and climate. But ironically,

* *Up the Organization.* New York: Alfred A. Knopf, 1970.

the most common management approach is closer to Theory X, even though companies that have adopted Theory Y have been able to attract and keep the best managers at a remarkably high productivity level.

Forecasting by the Facts

Another challenge the manager faces is to stop forecasting the future on the basis of the past. When the latter type of forecasting is done, the usual result is to identify and manage momentum rather than potential. Furthermore, rapid changes have made this extrapolative practice virtually obsolete.

The most common form of planning and decision making focuses on the objective as a starting point. The typical company plan is numbers-oriented, beginning with the sales forecast, supported by plans of action that require resources to accomplish, which are summarized in the budget; then the difference between the budget and the forecast becomes the profit plan.

This kind of planning approach may be used in a president's report to the board of directors:

> The company plans to sell $36 million worth of automotive parts to the automotive industry in 1975 at a total cost of $24 million, which includes $6 million of additional capital for inventory, in addition to an operating budget of $18 million, which means a profit plan of $12 million, which results in a satisfactory return on investment.

The plan looks good from a number of points of view, with a favorable profit and return on investment. But suppose the president had not researched the market. Suppose he just *assumed* that there was no competition, that his firm would have 100 percent market penetration, and that there would be 28 million cars produced. How valid would the forecast and profit plan be if only 14 million cars were produced and competition reduced his firm's share to 50 percent of the available market? Obviously, not valid at all. But the error would not be in the numbers or the objectives stated in the forecast; the error would be in the assumptions made and the facts not considered or inaccurately perceived.

The same type of error is made by a salesman who establishes a sales goal based on the assumption that a new product will be ready by a certain date, and then fails to confirm the accuracy of his assumption (or perhaps is unaware of the importance of his assumption to the validity of his forecast).

Correct identification of the present situation and sound judgment are the real determinants of how accurate a forecast will be. It is the quality of our thinking that determines the quality of our objectives. Also, it is the facts we use—and the guesstimates we make of a future we cannot predict with accuracy—that provide the standard for anticipating and measuring changes, not the objectives by themselves. Finally, it is in the ascertainment and consideration of these facts and judgments, as represented in the first three steps of the Planagement process, that true potentials are identified and strategy is born.

If we are to be able to identify and manage the existing potential and establish a sound direction, it is essential that we communicate the key factors used to develop the forecast and other objectives. To do this effectively requires adopting techniques and tools based on the Logic–Planagement process.

Part III

The Planagement System and Supporting Tools

7

Establishing
Sound Direction

In order to insure that the Planagement System would perform as needed, it was imperative that it:

1. Be in accordance with the processes described in Part II (principally the logic, management, and planning processes).
2. Meet the major individual, manager, and organization needs and the criteria used to measure results, as described in Chapter 4.
3. Establish a total management information system that could be used by people, organizational units, and the entire organization.
4. Integrate and simplify management concepts and programs into a single teachable system.
5. Contribute toward establishing a sound direction with enough flexibility to manage change and produce a constant gain.

A framework for the Planagement System was established. Still, there was no practical, teachable approach to convert the concept into reality. The primary stumbling block seemed to be related to the inability of managers to answer the fundamental question: *What is the minimum amount of information you require to make a sound decision, and in what order do you consider it?* It was believed that the answer would produce the insight needed to develop the Planagement System and meet the established criteria.

The Search for a Model

Research was commenced and several hundred managers, at all levels of management in a wide variety of companies, were asked the fundamental question. Dealing with it frustrated the average manager because, while he did not have a ready answer, he recognized that it was an important consideration. Practically all managers said they would give the question some thought and then submit their ideas.

Research was conducted over about a two-year period, and on the basis of the answers obtained, a model was evolved. This model was not comprised of data or answers, but rather of key questions and thought stimulators. Eventually it contained several hundred key questions. It was noticed that some of these questions were more basic than others, and that they tended to *cluster* around still more basic questions. Finally the model was related to the logic, management, and planning processes.

Assuming that the concept of Planagement was sound, this model would be the proper tool to meet or exceed the criteria the Planagement System was required to meet. In other words, the model of key questions and thought stimulators, which were arranged in a logical sequence, should rapidly produce a sound plan that could be reduced to writing by answering the questions contained in the model, and these questions should be applicable to any individual or manager, as well as to any organizational unit, type of organization, or situation.

When the model was applied by a management team, the results met the criteria—indeed, they exceeded expectations. The plan that evolved from applying the Planagement Model was submitted to management with an introduction that stated:

> We believe this plan is sound and, as pointed out, will almost double the return on investment over the next five years as compared to the present plan. We stand ready to be measured in accomplishing this plan and ask for your approval so we can make it happen.

The plan was thoroughly studied by top management, was approved, and became an operating reality.

Since this initial application, the Planagement Model has been used by several thousand people, usually with astounding results. It has been adopted as a management system by companies that range in size from a multibillion-dollar corporation with over 100,000 employees around the world, to a one-man proprietorship with less than $20,000 in sales. The Planagement System has been successfully applied by a seventh-grade drop-out on a Mississippi drilling rig and a group of Ph.D.'s who first used it to build a plan for their college and then offered the Planagement System as a course of instruction. The system works just as well for nonprofit organizations as it does for profit-oriented organizations because both need to establish sound direction in support of their missions.

It is not my purpose to detail the numerous successes that the Planagement System has achieved because I believe it would be of greater interest and benefit to you if you would test the value of the system for yourself. Real understanding is in the doing, and education is in the application. You may observe several hundred swimmers in action, read many books on swimming, and attend a number of lectures and demonstrations, but until you get into the water and begin to swim, you have not converted the concept of swimming into reality for yourself. So it is with the concept of Planagement. It will become a reality for you once you master the Planagement discipline through your own application of the Planagement techniques and tools.

The Planagement Model has been refined and reduced to the point where it is possible for anyone to create a guideline plan for himself, his job, and his future in a relatively short period of time. Presidents have developed a comprehensive guideline plan for their companies in a day, and management teams in two days.

This is astonishing when you consider that many people regularly involved in planning believe that the average time required to successfully implement a planning system in a medium size organization is from four to seven years. The primary reason it takes so much less time with the Planagement System is that the key questions that should be answered in any plan are made clear and structured in such a way that the plan will be developed through the written answers of those who are responsible for establishing it and making it an operating reality. Of course, like any tool, it is dependent on its user. In a sense, the Planagement tool can be compared to a good recipe. The quality of the ingredients and the skill of the cook determine in large measure the quality of the product.

Summary of the Planagement Model

To use the Planagement System to generate a beginning or guideline plan, it is not necessary, or particularly desirable, to go into the complete, detailed Planagement Model.* A summary of the model may be used; relatively little time is required for application.

Section 1

To do a situation analysis—to know where you are now—you need to gain an objective understanding of the existing situation as it relates to *you* as a person, your *business,* and your *function* within the business. There are several factors to consider:

How do you define yourself and your business?
What is your mission; what are the major results you wish to achieve?
What are your most important capabilities (or those of your business, function, or product)?

Other questions that should help define your business and function pertain to the nature of the business, its customers, key influences on sales, markets served and their needs, products and services, profit and performance history, present organization, and—very important—accountabilities.

This first section provides a good outline for establishing a business charter or a written job description. Actually, when a person uses the Planagement System to plan, manage, and control his job, he begins to view his job as a business and himself as general manager.

Section 2

The *external environment*—key trends in markets, technology, government, society, economics, and psychology—is an important part of the existing situation that must be considered. In addition, the *internal environment,* or climate, must be analyzed for the reasons discussed in Chapter 6.

Another significant factor is *competition.* It is important to know the competition's strengths, weaknesses, primary actions, and strategy in order to develop a plan and strategy to meet and defeat the competition—if your mission is to be the leader in your chosen field.

---

* A summary of the model is documented in the *Planagement Manual,* which would be used to develop an in-depth plan when the situation requires it. The *Planagement Manual* (Tulsa, Okla.: Planagement, Inc., 1970) is available from the publisher or from any licensed Planagement consultant, counselor, or educator.

But this is of secondary importance to your individual or organizational self-analysis because you and your organization have a unique potential that should be identified, managed, and achieved. Joe Batten, author of *Tough-Minded Management,** put this in perspective when he said, "An amateur competes against others; a professional competes against himself."

Finally to be considered are your or your organization's *key vulnerabilities,* together with the actions that might be taken to reduce or eliminate them.

Section 3

Once the basic facts have been identified, gathered, and written (Sections 1 and 2), you will need to analyze them and identify your most important existing *capabilities* and *opportunities.*

On the basis of numerous applications, the best analytical approach seems to be to relate your most important positive factors (*strengths* and *opportunities*) to your most important negative factors (*weaknesses* and *problems*) to evolve *alternative actions* that build on the positive and overcome the negative factors. When this analysis is completed, you should be in a good position to identify your important capabilities and opportunities in their order of importance, which will help you establish proper priorities.

When the first three sections are finished in written form, you will have completed the first three steps of the logic process (define and analyze the situation and develop alternatives). The subjects which should be considered for analysis would include key result areas, basic functional areas, managerial areas, markets, products, services, competition, organization, personnel, and some personal considerations as well.

Section 4

While each of the twelve sections in the Planagement System is important, the fourth section of your plan, which identifies *assumptions* and *potentials,* is perhaps the most crucial. In this section the facts that were identified in Sections 1–3 are combined with your judgment, experience, intuition, opinion, expertise, and guesstimates. Careful documentation of these assumptions and potentials is extremely important because of the difficulty of predicting the future in a period of dynamic change.

Whenever possible, an assumption should clearly state what is

* New York: AMACOM, 1963.

going to happen by when, and it should include the key factors that affect the accuracy of the assumptions. A common frame of reference and understanding should be established for all those involved in the plan. If the assumptions and potentials are written down, widely disseminated, and understood, the magnitude and direction of any changes that affect them will be more readily apparent. Also, this approach allows the manager to anticipate rather than just react, to prevent problems before they occur rather than solve them as they come up.

Among the more important assumptions and potentials that should be included in the fourth section of the plan are those that are basic to the business and its major objectives. These would include forecasts and key assumptions about support from others. The latter will help you ascertain how the informal organization works and will make greater delegation possible, since people will learn to communicate better with each other. Whenever a person agrees to support someone else's assumption, this will become an objective in his own plan, and he will report by exception if the objective needs to be changed. With this kind of modus operandi, management will be able to get things done through other people *regardless of reporting relationships.*

The types of potentials that should be considered in Section 4 are potentials for the business, organization, organizational unit, product, project, and individual. The most important potentials should be identified and ranked in order of importance.

It is in this fourth section of the plan that a sound strategy for the successful accomplishment of the entire plan will begin to emerge.

Section 5

Though this is the section where most planning starts (management by objectives), it is the contention of the Planagement System that the most important part of the plan is contained in the first four sections. It is the facts that are considered, along with the accuracy of those facts and how well they are analyzed and combined with judgment in Section 4, that will determine the soundness of the *objectives* or direction established in Section 5. Also, changes will occur in the facts, assumptions, and potentials, not in the objectives.

As noted before, the benefits associated with the management-by-objectives concept are based on the assumption that the objective is sound, and therefore we manage by and with assumptions and toward objectives.

An objective is a statement that clearly communicates *what* is going to happen by *when*. As observed in Chapter 5, a sound objective should be measurable, feasible, valuable, flexible, suitable, achievable, acceptable, and capable of eliciting commitment. To determine whether or not an objective meets these criteria, you will need to evaluate the information contained in the first four sections of the plan, as well as the information contained in Sections 6–12.

In order to insure that the Planagement-by-objectives program will succeed, these guidelines are suggested for your consideration and implementation:

1. Each objective should be developed and documented in writing by the person responsible for accomplishing it. It must be within his job responsibility and capability to attain.

2. Objectives should be submitted with the written plan that evolved them and a list of the actions that will make the objectives happen. The total plan should include the logic, facts, judgments, assumptions, actions, justifications, and key milestones for monitoring and feedback purposes.

3. Objectives should be related directly or indirectly to profit, growth, or other measurable gain (results).

4. Objectives should be responsive to, and supportive of, the overall objectives of the supervisor, the department, the function, the division, and the entire organization. Every objective should be reviewed with the supervisor and, following his acceptance, reported on by exception with agreed-on standards for judging performance, key milestones, and major changes that indicate the objective should be altered.

5. Objectives should be dynamic in nature. Enlargement of the objectives should be permitted (indeed, encouraged) in order to take advantage of expanding opportunities. The focus should be on preventing problems rather than on just solving them, on anticipating and managing change to advantage rather than on reacting to it. If the objectives challenge people to think and act beyond the routine duties of their jobs, they will contribute to continual job expansion and employees will grow as individuals.

6. Rewards (salary incentives) should be tied to the results achieved from the accomplishment of sound objectives.

7. The Planagement-by-objectives program should be part of a comprehensive and sound planning program that is practiced at all management levels. This program should integrate planning/management/organization/objectives/motivation/communication/development/control/and compensation into a single teachable

and easily practiced system. Such a systems approach will contribute to the establishment of sound objectives and the success of the Planagement program.

The types of objectives (goals) that should be considered in this fifth section of the plan are:

- Guideline objectives: Provided by the company, the organizational units, and the supervisor.
- Standard objectives: Same as a properly written standard of performance; often evolved from the accountabilities section of the job description, which should be included in Section 1 of the plan.
- Problem-solving objectives: A source for these is the third section of the plan.
- Innovative objectives: Personal objectives involving *novel* or non-recurring situations that require the development of *new concepts* and *imaginative approaches* will frequently emerge. These are the objectives that contribute to job enlargement.

Additional types of objectives which might be included in Section 5 are those relating to *support of others' assumptions* and the following key result areas: *customer satisfaction* (marketing and sales); *productivity* (output over input, including the manufacturing function); *innovation* (the future-oriented creativity of an organization or individual that results in new ventures management and the conversion of a personal hope or idea into reality); *resources* (allocation of resources to produce a sound balance between profit, profitability, and growth); *management development and performance* (a program that insures that the right person will be in the right job now and in the future); *employee attitudes and performance* (a climate that stimulates improved attitudes and performance); *public responsibility* (insuring that public, government, and community influences are favorable); *communications* (a clearly understood direction and a management information system that provides a common format so better decisions can be made faster); and finally, *profitability* (a continuing gain from the activity which results from an optimum balance of profit, growth, satisfaction, and just plain fun).

Once these and other objectives have been established in Section 5 of the plan, it is essential to rank them in order of importance. Clearly identify the most important objective and those relatively few basic objectives that will directly contribute toward achieving and controlling at least 80 percent of the anticipated results.

If the first five sections of the Planagement System are done correctly, then sound direction should be established. The completion of Section 5 of the plan will also complete the fourth step of the logic process, which is to make a decision. It is important to emphasize, however, that making a decision is secondary to making a *sound* decision that will establish a sound direction.

Section 6

This element of the Planagement System provides the *policy, procedures, and strategy* that make up the framework (guidance) for accomplishing the plan in the most effective way. Now we move from where we want to go (decision and direction) to how we are going to get there.

This is a vitally important section because the strategy chosen will probably determine 70 percent or more of the plan's chances of success. Policy, procedures, and strategy should be strongly consistent with the mission, and with the most important capability, opportunity, potential, and objective (as identified in Sections 3, 4, and 5 of the plan).

It would be well to review some suggested meanings of these vitally important terms. One common definition of policy is "a definite course or method of action selected from among various alternatives and in light of given conditions to guide and determine present and future decisions." Policy is a broad generalization that reflects the philosophy and mission of the organization. Procedures, on the other hand, are precise statements that define the operating steps to be taken. Strategy is a statement of how an activity should be approached. Usually it is more precise than a policy and is commonly related to a specific activity. A statement of strategy should still be general enough to allow specific supporting action plans to be developed—for example, to support the organization's objective for growth *primarily through internal development as opposed to acquisition.* A wide variety of strategies should be considered; several are reviewed in Chapter 9.

Section 6 completes the strategic part of the plan, which now must be supported by actions required to make the plan happen.

Section 7

This is the action part of the plan. It contains *programs, projects,* and the key *alternatives* basic to contingency planning.

Programs and projects are the documented plans of action that indicate the activity required to make the objective happen. Programs are usually broader in scope and are composed of several projects.

Ideally, the plans of action will be presented in an organized manner so that the minimum amount of information necessary for a sound decision will be provided. The Planagement Project Data Form (PA5A) has been created to assist you in ascertaining the essential elements of information. (See Figure 1.) It is one of the most important tools in support of the Planagement process.

Because some changes are likely, it is well to construct alternative plans of action (contingency planning). Then when a change does occur, an alternate course of action that has been prepared in advance can be rapidly implemented.

Section 7 is vitally important to Planagement because it is here that the strategic plan is integrated with the operations plan. The greatest idea in the world will not be of much use unless it is backed up by the solid, consistent, and persistent actions required to make it happen.

When Section 7 of the Planagement Model is accomplished, you will have completed the identification of the actions to be taken to make the plan happen (the fifth step of the logic process). Then you will be in a position to summarize and soundly modify the plan according to what is wanted and what is possible. This summary of the plan identifies the basic resources needed to accomplish it—including time, people, money, materials, and gain generated—and will demonstrate whether the plan is practical and desirable or an albatross. Naturally, the latter conclusion would be disappointing to the planners, managers, and everyone else who spent time on the plan, but it is far better to gauge results now so you can scrap a bad plan than to casually implement it and deal with disastrous consequences later.

The summary of resources is contained in Sections 8, 9, 10, and 11. The gain or loss is dependent on the soundness of the decisions made and the strategy established, as well as on the efficiency of the plans of action.

Section 8

Now you must establish *priorities* and *schedules* (when the plan will be accomplished and the timing of key milestones that are essential to this accomplishment). Since there are seldom resources to do everything you want to do, it is essential that you determine the priority of your objectives and then make up an operational schedule form showing this order of priority. The schedule should also in-

Figure 1. Planagement project data form (PA5A).

	THIS	REPLACES
FILE:		
DATE:		
PAGE:	OF	OF

OBJECTIVE/PROJECT SUMMARY

I. OBJECTIVE (What and When):

II. ASSUMPTION(S)/POTENTIALS:

III. STRATEGY (How) (Plan of Action):

  A. Programs/Projects (Approach) (Plan of Action):

  B. Schedule (When):

  C. Responsibility (Who):

  D. Resources:

    1. Money:

    2. Manpower:

    3. Others:

  E. Purpose/Results (Why):

  F. Alternatives Considered (Description and Disposition):

    1. Contingency:

    2. Others:

dicate the projected dates of completion of the objectives and the supportive key programs, projects, and/or milestones. Critical-path techniques or PERT charts and/or Gantt charts may be incorporated.

If possible, also incorporate in this section of the plan a flow chart that is an overall picture of the plan, showing what is going to happen, when it is going to happen, and the interrelationship and importance of the key factors in the plan. If this is done in a quantified way, then you might also be able to create a model of the plan that utilizes the computer.

In addition to the above factors, it would be advisable to show the timing of key decision making, as well as the timing for required additional resources over and above the approved operating budget—including additional invested capital that exceeds the cash flow generated by the plan.

Section 9

The ninth section of the plan is concerned with *organization, delegation,* and *development* (who is going to do what).

Management has often been defined as the art and science of getting things done through other people. To accomplish this, you must have an appropriate organization that is compatible with and supportive of your plan.

A key principle of the Planagement System is that the growth and development of the organization are directly dependent on the growth and development of the people who comprise the organization. One way to successfully develop employees is to delegate the maximum possible responsibility and authority. Planagement considers every employee with other than routine responsibility and/or routine ambition as a planning/management center, and assists him to better understand his own potential and how it may be related to his job, the organization, and his future. Therefore Planagement is an individual as well as a management and organization development program.

Section 9 integrates the concepts of organization, delegation, and development into a program of building on human resources so that the right person is in the right job, at the right time, at the proper cost. This is essential to a sound planning program and to maximizing profits, growth, and satisfaction because plans are only as sound as the people who create them and who have the responsibility for making them work.

The first elements to be included in this section are the recommended organization structure for implementing the plan and the descriptions of jobs and talents needed to effectively and efficiently support the organization. Once these elements are established, the guidelines for manpower planning and development should be clearly identified for both the short term and the long term. These guidelines will provide the criteria for a tailored development and training program that capitalizes on the potentials and ambitions of the people involved with the plan.

Section 10

This section of the Planagement Model identifies and documents the *budgets* and *resources* required to accomplish the plan. Cost is estimated and measured against how much the organization is willing and able to pay to accomplish the plan. Unless the approved plan is supported by the needed men, money, material, time, and space, it will fail totally or in part.

The documentation of the budgets and resources should include the current operating budget, profit and loss statement, capital budget, balance sheet, cash flow, return on investment, assets employed and return on those assets, planning gap statements based on the difference between what is wanted and what is possible, and all other quantitative and qualitative resources required to accomplish the plan.

Sections 6–10 identify and summarize the actions necessary to the plan and their cost, and correspond to Step 5 of the logic process, which is to take action.

Section 11

In this section of the plan, the gain from the activity is summarized in the form of *justifications, results,* and *profitability.* The benefit from the plan is identified and compared to the costs (as summarized in Section 10), thus providing the basis for a cost/benefit analysis.

All too often the primary reasons for planning are forgotten or misunderstood. Some managers become so immersed in the practice of the art and science of management that they consider the plan and its implementation more important than the profit, product, business, or individual growth the plan is supposed to promote. It is the purpose of Section 11 to remind you of the basic reasons behind plans and programs for business and business management, and the need to justify those reasons (Step 6 of the logic process).

This is the section in which the value of the organization's growth is identified. One definition of this growth might be "to achieve a return on the assets (resources) already committed that will be sufficient to attract the new assets required to accomplish the plan." This section could contain reason sheets, cost savings, payouts, results, guidelines, feasibility studies, and comments on contributions to profitability, plus justifications for the activity or business in general and new recommendations and their justifications.

Section 12

This section is actually outside the plan, which has been completed in the previous eleven sections. Section 12, however, is essential to a living plan.

The dynamic tool that completes the closed loop—that keeps the plan constantly current—is called the *exception report*. It corresponds to the seventh step of the logic process, which is to redefine the situation as change requires.

One of the Planager's biggest challenges is to manage change well. On the one hand, he has the responsibility of accomplishing his plan. On the other, he must take care that the plan is kept in tune with any changes that might have an impact on it.

In order to reduce paperwork and keep the time spent on the mechanics of planning to an absolute minimum, the managing and reporting by exception concept is utilized. The exception report should include the present plan together with past, present, and anticipated changes that will affect the plan, adjustments to be made, expected results, and the impact of those results on the plan. The updated pages of the plan should be attached to the exception report. Naturally, the exception report should be approved by all those who are affected by the exception, especially the immediate supervisor who approved the plan.

Miscellaneous/Reference Planning Section

This section, while not part of the Planagement Model, can be useful for collecting information that relates to your job and your plan, and for incorporating existing or needed reports required to make decisions.

It is important to keep the Planagement Model as free as possible of anything not specifically needed to manage your plan or to make necessary operating decisions for your area of responsibility. As material becomes obsolete, delete it. Information that is no longer dynamic but is still desirable for reference should be transferred to planning files whose sections and logical order are the same as those in your plan.

Items that might be included in this section are coordination reports, exception reports from others that affect your plan, activity reports, sales reports, and copies of plans of others that are basic to your own plan.

The Planagement Matrix

Now you have the summary of the Planagement Model. With this model, it is possible to complete the Planagement Matrix, which goes from the concept, as represented by the logic process, to the Planagement System, as described in this chapter. (See Table 5.) The Planagement System integrates many normally fragmented management concepts and programs into a single, comprehensive system, as illustrated in Table 6.

Planagement Checklist for Sound Decision Making

1. Establish the facts as they exist now and write them down in logical sequence (Sections 1 and 2).

2. Analyze these facts by classifying them as positive or negative ones, and evolve alternative actions that might be taken to build on the positive facts and overcome the negative ones (Section 3).

3. Make your best guesstimates about a future you probably can't predict with accuracy by writing down your assumptions and potentials (Section 4). Remember, exceptions or changes are likely.

4. From your choices, evolve objectives that clearly state what will happen by when. Put these objectives in order of priority, noting the most important (Section 5).

5. Develop a broad strategy for accomplishing your objectives. It has been estimated that 70 percent of your success will be determined by the soundness of your strategy and the strategic plan, which you have just completed (Section 6).

6. Establish the plans of action that are required to make the objectives happen, together with the key steps (milestones) that must be taken, by whom and when, in order to accomplish the objectives within the specified time (Section 7).

7. Summarize the resources you require to achieve the objectives, including time (priorities and schedules, Section 8), people (organization, delegation, and development, Section 9), and money (budgets/resources, Section 10).

Table 5. Planagement matrix.

STEPS	LOGIC PROCESS	PLANAGEMENT PROCESS	MANAGEMENT PROCESS
1	Define the situation	Logic/facts/belief (science)	Plan
2	Analyze the situation	Analysis/alternatives (science and art)	Plan
3	Evolve alternatives	Judgments/ assumptions/ potentials (art)	Plan and organize
4	Decide	Decision/objectives (direction)	Organize
5	Take action	Plan of action (discipline)	Implement
6	Justify; know why	Why/justification (gain from the activity)	Control
7	Identify deviations	Control/exceptions/ update/deviations/ changes (living plan)	Control/update
The steps needed to make a decision and to make that decision a reality.	Process is repeated continuously. This is the process of the mind—the common-sense process.	Plan your work; work your plan; change plan as necessary Closed-loop systems approach.	Basic functions of professional management: to consistently manage inconsistent situations in such a way as to produce constant gain from the activity.

PLANNING PROCESS	CHECKLIST QUESTIONS	PLANAGEMENT SYSTEM	PLANAGEMENT MANUAL SECTIONS BASED ON THE MODEL
Where you are now; what you are now	What	Define business/function	Section 1
		Define environment/ competition	Section 2
Where you are now; what you are now	What	Analyze capabilities Analyze strengths/ opportunities Analyze weaknesses/ problems	Section 3
Where you are now; what you are now; where you want to go	What	Evolve alternative actions	Section 3
	Where	Assumptions/ potentials	Section 4
Where you want to go	Where	Decide: assumptions/ potentials	Section 4
		Decide: objectives	Section 5
How you will get there; when you expect to arrive; who is going to do what	How	Policy/procedures/ strategy	Section 6
	How	Programs/ projects/ alternatives	Section 7
	When	Priorities/ schedules	Section 8
	Who	Organization/ delegation/ development	Section 9
How much you will pay; why you are going		Budgets/ resources (cost)	Section 10
	Why	Justification/why/ results (benefits)	Section 11
How you are doing	Change	Exception report	Section 12
Basic steps of the planning process as related to planning a trip.	The six basic questions that *identify* are those which ask what, where, how, when, who, and why.	Identify—to tailor and apply. Implement—to understand. Audit—to measure. Living plan concept.	What, where, how, when, who, and why. Continuously update through exception reporting.

Table 6. The Planagement System integrates the major programs used by today's management.

SECTION OF THE PLANAGEMENT MODEL AND SYSTEM	MAJOR MANAGEMENT PROGRAMS
1 Business/function	Planning, organization development, accountability management (position description), skills inventory
2 Environment/competition	Planning, climate management
3 Capabilities/opportunities	Planning, analysis, alternatives
4 Assumptions/potentials	Planning, decision making, judgment, future expectations
5 Objectives	Management by objectives, management development, salary administration, creativity, key results
6 Policies/procedures/ strategy	Strategic planning
7 Programs/projects/ alternatives	Operational and contingency planning
8 Priorities/schedules	Planning, monitoring, and controlling
9 Organization/delegation/ development	Organization and management development, self-development, manpower planning, salary administration, training, right person/right job
10 Budgets/resources	Budgets and control, key operating and results ratios
11 Justifications/results/ profitability	Planning and control, management of results, profitability management, basis for compensation
12 Exception report	Control, measuring performance, management development, salary administration, replanning (the living plan), management by exception, management information system, job enlargement and enrichment, management of time, management of change

8. Determine the gains (results) expected from your plan in the form of profit (a specific gain achieved), profitability (a continuing gain from your activity), and growth (your increased capabilities from a continuous program of self-development) (Section 11).

9. Identify and manage changes (exceptions) that affect your plan (Section 12). A living plan will allow you to achieve, or even increase, the benefits anticipated. It is a continuous, closed-loop, never-ending system.

8

Do It, Do It Now, Do It Right Now

THE FIRST seven chapters described the needs and criteria the Planagement System was designed to meet. Using the logic process, we evolved the Planagement process, which we in turn used to build the supporting Planagement Model. It was emphasized that in order to really understand the Planagement System, you must apply it to yourself, your job, and your future.

In this chapter you are requested to begin to apply the Planagement System by answering some key questions that will assist you in developing objectives. The primary purpose is to get you to experience the Planagement discipline, and through it to begin to develop sound direction supported by written objectives.

The first question you must resolve is *where you are now*, which includes the most important facts, the analysis of those facts, and the development of alternative actions. To answer this question, use the first three sections of your plan, referred to as a situation analysis.

Section 1: Business and Function

Write down your answers to these questions:

- What plan do you intend to create? Define your plan with regard to whether it is based on yourself, your job, your ca-

reer, a major opportunity or problem, or any combination of these.
- What is your mission or primary purpose? State the major result you wish to achieve.
- What are your most important capabilities, resources, and primary skills?
- What have been your most important recent accomplishments?
- What are your most important accountabilities; how do you measure your performance on each accountability; and what percent of your total available time do you spend on each accountability?

A brief example of how this first section of the plan might be written follows.

Salesman's Plan—Section 1

This plan is for my *job* as a salesman.

My *personal mission* is to grow as a manager to the point of being promoted into sales management and, eventually, general management. The primary *mission* in my job is to establish a sales volume and market penetration that will put me in the top 10 percent of the company's sales force.

The most important *capability* I have is getting along well with people. My most important *resources* are an excellent product line, a growing market, and a company that enjoys a good reputation. My primary *skills* are selling, communication, and administration.

Major recent *accomplishments* are increasing sales volume by 20 percent each of the last two years, establishing an average of five new accounts each quarter, and increasing market penetration from 10 to 15 percent.

My most important *accountabilities* are sales, as measured by sales volume (80 percent of my time); and paperwork, as measured by accurate, on-time reports submitted in accordance with company requirements (15 percent of my time). In addition, I feel I am accountable for improving myself and my performance, so I allow 5 percent of my time for self-development and I measure my performance by increases in compensation and promotions.

Section 2: Environment and Competition

The questions you should answer in writing this section of your plan include:

- What are the major external environmental factors and trends that are having an impact on you and your plan?
- What are the key considerations in your internal environment that are affecting you, your performance, and your plan?
- What is the competitive situation?
- What is your most important vulnerability or threat, and what action can you take to reduce or eliminate it?

While there are several other questions that could, and possibly should, be asked in this section, these four are the most important for identifying the environment and competition.

Salesman's Plan—Section 2

The trend in the *external environment* that is having the greatest impact on me and my plan is high interest rates, which are causing some of my customers to place their business where they can get the best financial terms, or to lease their equipment rather than purchase it. Another significant trend is the slowdown of the market I serve from a past annual growth rate of 10 percent to an annual growth of about 5 percent. In addition, the poor economic climate and fear of a depression is causing a cut-back of purchases or indecision on the part of many customers I serve.

The *internal environment* is healthy in that I am confident I can meet or beat my forecast, and there is a good possibility for me to advance in the company if I perform well.

Competition is increasing; there are three additional salesmen in my territory and they are presently offering more attractive financial terms than we are. However, our product line is preferred by the customers, as they feel it is superior.

The *key vulnerability* I face is that if our product line loses its superiority, it will adversely affect my ability to sell it and continue to increase our market penetration. The *action* I must take to reduce this vulnerability is to continue to provide our research and development department with up-to-date information on our customers' needs and competitors' changes in their product line.

Section 3: Capabilities and Opportunities

Now that the first two sections of your plan have been completed, you have identified and written down the important facts. Your next step is to analyze these facts and evolve alternative actions. It is suggested that you use the related analysis approach, as this will allow you to develop actions that capitalize on positive factors and reduce or overcome negative factors in the business, function, and/or the environment. In writing the third section of your plan, include:

- Your most important strengths (capabilities) as related to your most important weaknesses, and the alternative actions that could be taken to build on your strengths and overcome your weaknesses.
- Your most important opportunities as related to your most important problems, and the alternative actions that could be taken.
- Relate your most important capability (strength) to your most important opportunity and the most important action that could be taken to build on the strength and capitalize on the opportunity.

Once you have completed this section (see the sample plan in Table 7), you should have established where you are now and have gained some insight into what kinds of action you will consider in Sections 4 and 5 of your plan.

Section 4: Assumptions and Potentials

In this section you will identify where you want to go, which is the first phase of your decision-making process. After you identify the most important potentials you want to manage, you will gain insight into the strategy you might employ to realize them. Some of the questions you should answer in writing are:

- What are the most important assumptions you are making in regard to your plan?
- What are your most important potentials, in order of value, and what action should you take to realize these potentials?

Salesman's Plan—Section 4

The most important *assumptions* I am making in this plan are that our product will remain superior to the competition's for at least the next five years, and that I will be promoted to district manager within the next four years if I meet or exceed my three-year forecast, which has been reviewed and approved by management.

The most important *potential* is the 85 percent of the market not presently being served by our product line. Each one percent of the market has an estimated value of $100,000, and therefore the poten-

Table 7. Salesman's plan—Section 3.

STRENGTHS	WEAKNESSES	ACTIONS
Get along with people, selling skill	Sales-oriented rather than management-oriented position	Study management and learn management job through performance as a salesman—self-development program
Superior product line	Competition is increasing	Advise research and development department of customer needs and competitive changes; establish more new accounts

OPPORTUNITIES	PROBLEMS	ACTIONS
85% of the market is not sold by me	Lack of time to cover the market, plus increasing competitive strength because there are more salesmen in the field	Establish a key account program; use direct mail as a supplement to personal sales calls
To increase sales volume	Market growth is slowing; economy is poor; competitors' financing plans are superior	Emphasize superiority of product and provide the customer with a cost/benefit analysis

STRENGTH	OPPORTUNITY	ACTIONS
Superior product line	85% of the market remains to be sold this product	Establish a key account program; supplement personal sales efforts with direct mail campaign

tial additional sales volume is $8.5 million. The *action* I will take is to establish a key account program that will identify the 20 percent of the customers who would account for around 80 percent of this total potential, and concentrate 80 percent of my sales time on them.

Section 5: Objectives

Objectives are statements of what you will do by when. Some of the questions you should answer in writing Section 5 are:

- What are your most important standard objectives? These objectives should be evolved primarily from your job accountabilities.

- What is your most important problem-solving objective? Section 3 is a source for this, as are the negative factors identified in Section 2.
- What is your most important innovative and/or personal objective?
- What is your most important objective and why is it the most important?

When you complete this section of your plan, you should have established a sound, clear direction, as represented by the objectives you have written down.

In order to check the soundness of your objectives, the following guide is suggested. If you can answer yes to these questions, then the chances are excellent that your objectives are sound.

1. Are your objectives feasible—can they be accomplished?
2. Can you measure your objectives—do they clearly state what is to be done by when?
3. Are your objectives suitable—do they support the guideline objectives of your organization and your supervisor?
4. Will your objectives be acceptable—will they be approved and will the resources you require be provided?
5. Are your objectives flexible enough to accommodate change and firm enough to provide needed direction and an objective measurement of performance?
6. Are your objectives achievable—can they be accomplished through your own efforts?
7. Are you committed to making your objectives happen—are you challenged by them?
8. What values are to be gained from accomplishing your objectives—are they clearly identified?
9. Are your most important objectives consistent with your most important strengths, opportunities, and potentials?
10. Have you included all the key actions identified in the first four sections of your plan as objectives in Section 5?

In reviewing Section 5 of the salesman's plan, check the soundness of his objectives against the above guide. To do this, you will need to review the first four sections of his plan—which confirms why the process that evolved the objectives should be included with the objectives themselves in one plan.

Salesman's Plan—Section 5

My *standard objectives* are: to meet or exceed my sales forecast of $180,000 in 19xx, $220,000 in 19xx + 1, and $270,000 in 19xx + 2; to develop a new report form by June 1, 19xx, that will provide needed information to R&D and submit this report once each quarter, or more often, if required; to attend at least one management development program each year and complete at least one book or home study course on management each quarter, starting October 1, 19xx.

My most important *problem-solving objective* is to use my time more effectively through the establishment of a key account program by July 31, 19xx, and to increase market penetration at a more rapid rate.

My most important *innovative objective* is to earn a promotion to district manager by December 31, 19xx + 3, as a result of my performance (as measured by meeting or exceeding my forecast) and my management/self-development program.

My *most important objective* is to earn a promotion to district manager by December 31, 19xx + 3, because all other objectives are in support of this objective, which is in support of personal and job missions.

When you have completed the fifth section of your plan, you will have made your decision on where you want to go and have established your direction on the basis of the opportunities and potentials you have identified. You are now in a good position to manage your potential through the accomplishment of your objectives.

The question that must be answered now is, how are you going to accomplish your objectives? The answer will come out of the strategy you establish, together with the actions you plan to use to make your objectives happen.

9

The Vital Importance of Strategy

WHAT IS strategy? It is a term we frequently hear and use, but few of us seem to know precisely what it means.

Many leading businessmen and educators feel that sound strategy is essential to establishing a successful business, that it determines at least 70 percent of a business's future success and position in its field. It is thus surprising that few organizations have a written strategy. The general absence of a defined strategy is not due to ignorance of its importance, but rather to a failure to understand the concept of strategy and the process for developing sound strategy. In this chapter I will give you a workable definition of strategy, illustrate it with several examples, and suggest a process that should help you create a strategy for your plan.

As a starting point, let's examine some dictionary definitions of strategy: "the science and art of employing the political, economic, psychological, and military forces of a nation or group of nations to afford the maximum support to adopted policies in peace or war; the science and art of military command exercised to meet the enemy in combat under advantageous conditions; a careful plan or method; the art of devising or employing plans or stratagems toward a goal."

While the dictionary definitions emphasize the use of strategy by the military, it is just as applicable to business organizations, which develop plans and goals to meet the competition in the marketplace under advantageous conditions.

Several key words appear in these definitions. First, strategy is both an *art* and a *science.* This means that both judgment and a scientific process are involved. Next, strategy involves *political, economic,* and *psychological* factors, all of which are fundamental to building and running an organization. And certainly one of management's prime goals is to create a climate that will afford the *maximum support* to *adopted policies.*

Basically, strategy is the broad picture of how a goal will be accomplished, while tactics are the specific plans of action that will achieve that goal within the framework of the established strategy. Strategy is identifying the *right things to do;* tactics is *doing things right.*

Example 1—Military

During World War II, the story goes, General Douglas MacArthur was faced with the challenge of capturing 15 islands in a chain infested with enemy soldiers. It was estimated that each and every one of these islands would require several months to capture and cost thousands of American lives.

The tactics were clearly understood. First, an island would be bombed from the air, then from the sea. Next, troops would be landed to fight for ground—cave by cave, hill by hill—until the enemy was killed or surrendered.

The best military minds were put to work to establish a strategy that would reduce the terrible cost in lives, time, and other resources, yet achieve the crucial objective of capturing the 15 islands. After studying the facts (scientific analysis), the planners observed that the islands formed a chain, and it was their judgment (art of devising a strategy) that if every third island was captured, the intervening two would be starved into submission and neutralized. The strategy became one of taking every third island in the chain and fighting only 5 battles instead of the 15 originally scheduled. As a result, at least two-thirds of the originally needed resources—men, money, material, and time—were saved and the objective was achieved.

Example 2—Large Retailers

At one time Sears and Montgomery Ward were virtually equals in the retail field. Then the two leaders of these companies made a judgment on the United States economy. The chief executive officer of Montgomery Ward assumed that there would be a recession, and the company strategy became one of nonexpansion and preservation of ample corporation funds in a liquid state. The head of Sears, on the other hand, assumed that the economy would be growing, and his company's strategy became one of expansion.

Today, Sears is by far the leader in its field. The relative positions of these two giants in the retail field are due, in large measure, to the strategy adopted at that crucial time in their histories.

Example 3—Automotive Industry

Ford and General Motors were co-leaders in the automotive field many years ago. Both top management teams established the goal of gaining undisputed leadership, but they made very different assumptions on the basis of their research (and lack of it), and consequently developed two entirely different strategies.

Ford assumed that what the public wanted was the best-engineered, highest-quality automobile that could be built, and its strategy was to create the Lincoln Continental. Part of the reason for this decision was that the company was very engineering/production/sales oriented. General Motors, on the other hand, assumed (on the basis of market research) that what the public wanted was prestige, and this strategy was reflected in the image created for the Cadillac.

The result was that many more Cadillacs were sold than Lincolns, and this contributed to establishing GM as the leader in its field.

The Strategy Process

The process for developing strategy can be summarized in the following steps:

1. *Science:* Gather the appropriate facts and analyze them to evolve the best possible situation that can be established with the facts available.

2. *Art:* Apply judgment in the form of assumptions and establish potentials based on the facts in Step 1 and the assumptions made.

3. *Decision:* Steps 1 and 2 should contribute to making a decision as to what you wish to accomplish by when. This is the statement of an objective.

4. *Strategy:* Develop and identify the strategy by which you will accomplish the objective and state the general direction you wish to take in achieving the objective.

5. *Action plan:* Establish the plans of action (tactics) in the form of projects designed to accomplish the objective in the best way possible in order to maximize results. These plans of action include: steps needed to be taken (what is to be done), by whom and when (key milestones), resources required (cost), and results to be achieved (cost/benefit). These projects should be consistent with the strategy established.

The Strategy Process Applied

1. *Fact:* Company X is No. 3 in its field with a market share of 10 percent. An analysis of the facts indicates Company X has a superior technical capability and sales force.

2. *Judgment:* It is assumed that Company X can make an improved product, and that its sales force has the capability to increase its market share once it can sell the improved product.

3. *Decision:* It is decided that Company X will establish a leadership position in the field by obtaining at least a 50 percent share of the market by December 31, 19xx.

4. *Strategy:* The strategy established, based on the facts, judgment, and decision, is "to accomplish the objective through internal development rather than acquisition from the outside." A second strategy is designed to improve the company's profit position by and through "a greater participation in the markets it serves and maximum use of all resources employed in the business through effective planning, organization, and measurement of performance."

5. *Action Plan:* Project sheets are then developed in support of the objective. For example:

What: To complete the development of Product X
Who: Vice-president of R&D
When: March 15, 19xx
Resources: Personnel: Three people full time, plus 70 percent of the vice-president's time
            Money: $25,000
            Material: Two-thirds of R&D facility full time
Why: To increase market share by at least 10 percent each of the next four years

Strategy of Marketing versus Sales

Another illustration of the practical application of strategy is in determining whether to utilize a marketing or a sales approach. Many managers use the terms *marketing* and *sales* interchangeably, yet these terms have very different meanings and the application of one or the other produces vastly different results.

Marketing is that *continuous process* that provides an organization with the capability to correctly identify, anticipate, and communicate its market's *needs,* while organizing and utilizing the company's *resources* in such a manner that the firm will meet these needs as well as or better than anyone else, and at the same time achieve *optimum profits* and *growth.* The orientation of marketing is *outside/inside.* The nature of marketing is *long-range;* it involves *strategic thinking* and focuses on being *effective*—that is, doing the right things. (See Figure 2.)

Obviously, marketing is much broader than sales because it encompasses the sales function as well as the distribution and other functions. A marketing plan provides guidance for product development, engineering, and manufacturing. In a marketing-oriented company, these divisions are charged with the responsibility of continuously organizing and utilizing the resources of the company so that it will be able to meet the needs of its market as well as, or better than, its competitors, while achieving optimum profits and growth.

I do not mean to imply that marketing is the most important function. My purpose is merely to illustrate the sequence of functional events in a marketing-oriented organization.

Now to a definition of sales: *Sales* is that *process* which *maximizes demand* for the organization's products, processes, services, and other existing capabilities, and provides these to the served customers in the greatest possible *volume* at the highest possible *price.* The orientation of sales is *inside/outside.* The nature of sales is *short-range;* it emphasizes *tactical doing* and focuses primarily on being *efficient*—that is, doing things right. (See Figure 3.)

It was emphasized in an earlier chapter that we are living in an age where change is the only constant. The only three things we know for sure about the future are that it will not be like the past, it will not be what we think it is going to be, and the rate of change will be more rapid than ever before. Therefore, those companies that best anticipate and meet the needs of their markets and manage change to advantage will probably obtain a larger market share than those companies which sell only what they have and have had.

The rate of obsolescence is so rapid today that some believe the average life cycle of a product is now about three years, whereas in the past it was seven years or longer. Because of this constantly changing situation, many companies and managers are establishing a strategically oriented marketing concept and developing their man-

Figure 2. A flow diagram of marketing.

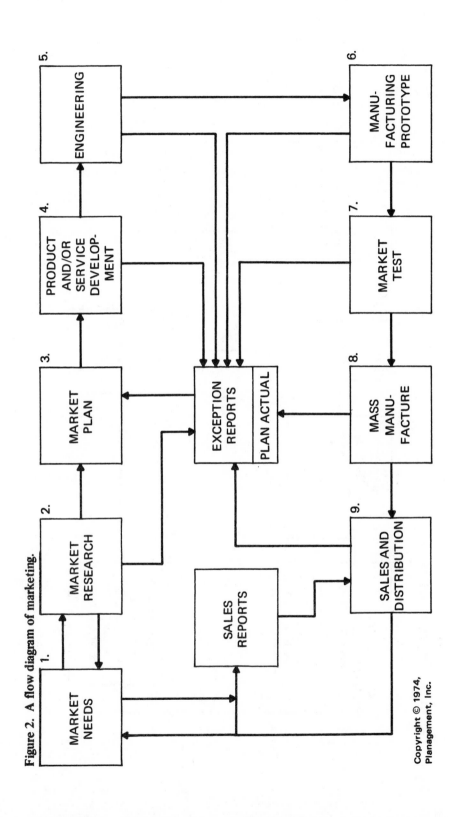

Figure 3. A flow diagram of sales.

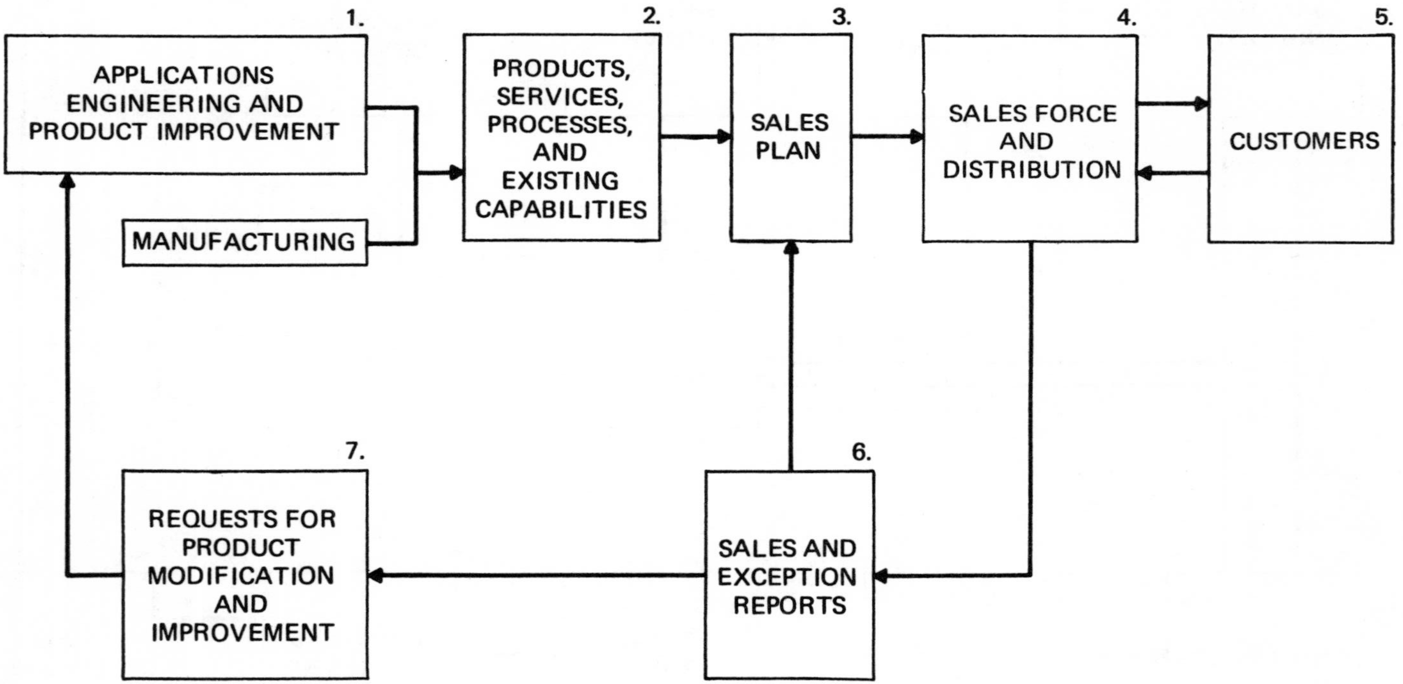

agement practices with the idea of implementing the marketing approach. The marketing approach seems more relevant today because it is oriented from the outside to the inside, is strategic (long-range) in nature, and is a continuous process of anticipation of needs and organization to meet those needs better. Companies that understand and master the marketing concept have a better opportunity to become leaders in their field. Those companies that are strictly sales-oriented tend to deal with the tomorrows much the same as they did with the yesterdays—usually by crisis management based on an acquired ability to react to change.

Strategy of Growth

One of the crucial areas that should be carefully considered in developing the organization's strategic plan is growth. First of all, growth should be defined. The normal definitions—increased sales, profits, and return on investment—are not satisfactory because all three could be accomplished by selling assets until the organization disappears up its own balance sheet. Your definition of growth should be to increase the assets you employ while improving the return on those assets so that you can attract and keep all the assets you require to accomplish your plan. Assets would include personnel, money, materials, time, and space.

Now you can proceed to establish a strategy for accomplishing growth according to your plan. For example: "To support the organization's objective for growth primarily through internal development as opposed to acquisition."

Strategy of Information Management and Control

Because of the information explosion discussed earlier, it is virtually mandatory to develop a strategy for managing and controlling information so that the minimum data required for sound decision making are identified, organized, and presented.

This need for information management raises the interesting question: What is the minimum amount of information you need to make a sound decision, and in what order should you consider this information?

A manager who can answer this difficult question on a consistent basis has mastered one of management's most sought after skills—the ability to recognize the key elements that effectively control the area for which he is responsible.

There seems to be an unwritten law that 10 to 20 percent of the elements in a situation control 80 to 90 percent of the results. Put another way: If we can identify the key control factors in a business, we can take better and more rapid action because we will have 10 to 20 basic things to do rather than 80 or 90.

Most people have a tendency to make the simple complex, and the complex hopelessly confusing. The advantages of reversing this process are enormous. There are several steps you can take to identify basics so that you can more effectively control your business or job.

The first is to develop and apply a systematic approach for identifying, gathering, organizing, and presenting the minimum amount of information required to make better decisions faster. This system, as discussed in previous chapters, is based on the logic process, the "common sense" everyone has been blessed with.

A serious problem in management is that managers do not allow themselves the proper time to think, partly because of pressure but to a great extent because they prefer being immersed in activity. An aura of busyness seems to be the most popular criterion for judging a person's work. But the constantly toiling manager may be doing many things over and over again instead of doing the right things the first time around. This brings us to the second suggested step, which is to list the most important elements in your job and business in order of priority.

This discipline of selecting the most important elements seems obvious and simple, yet for some reason it is infrequently applied. If you experiment by drawing up a priority list of the 100 things you have to manage or do, you will find that after the first 10 to 20 have been accomplished, the remainder will be taken care of much more easily and quickly. Still, most managers seem content with being pressured by the 100 and trying to do everything at once—usually taking five years to accomplish what might have been done better in one year.

Key Results

An extremely productive concept in assisting us to do the most important things first was developed by Peter Drucker, one of management's leading educators. Drucker has identified what he terms the key result areas of a business. On the basis of his own research and practice, he has concluded that if a manager manages these key result areas as well as or better than his competitors, he will be able to increase profitability. If he does not manage these key result areas as well as his competitors, then he will not achieve acceptable profitability.

The seven key result areas are: customer satisfaction, productivity, innovation, resources, management development and performance, employee attitudes and performance, and public responsibility. I suggest you add communications, climate management, and organization development to this important list.

Besides developing objectives in each of these areas, it is important to support the objectives with key result area strategies. Examples of these statements of strategies would be as follows:

Customer satisfaction: The company will adopt a marketing orientation and measure its progress in this key result area by market penetration and key account share.

Productivity: Each job will have at least five primary standards of performance, which will be measurable and measurably increased each year.

Innovation: Each manager and supervisor in the company will spend at least 10 percent of his time in innovative activity, with the overall result that at least 15 percent of the annual volume and profits of the company will come from products and services not in being three years before.

Resources: Organization growth will be measured by the increase in assets employed in the business, and the increase in the return on the assets employed.

Management development and performance: Each manager will have a written plan for his job, which will include a personal career plan supported by a program for self-development.

Employee attitudes and performance: Every six months each manager will conduct a performance/development review for those people reporting directly to him.

Public responsibility: A contribution budget will be developed and administered locally rather than centrally.

Communications: The company will establish a manager for communications. Reporting on plans will be primarily according to the exception report principle and procedure.

Climate management: The company will establish a positive internal climate based on Theory Y, as developed by Dr. Douglas McGregor in *The Human Side of Enterprise.*

Organization development: The company will establish an entrepreneurial type of organization structure, with the individual as the planning, management, control center for his area of responsibility.

In addition to these general key result areas (which apply to almost every company and management job), you might identify through applying Steps 1 and 2 of the strategy process up to ten additional key result areas that are important to your own business. The chances are that those 20 areas will control at least 80 percent or more of the results you are after.

Strategy in the Approach Taken to Planning

While there are many basic approaches to planning, two opposite methods are most frequently used by companies. The predominant one is the "budget backwards," highly numbers-oriented approach defined in the right column of Table 8. The Planagement approach is defined in the left column of the table.

Obviously, in practice, the approach used is not as black and white as Table 8 suggests; however, all organizations lean toward one or the other approach, depending on the style and training of the key management team, particularly the chief executive officer and his financial officer. There is now emerging a "creative controller" type of financial officer who is successfully integrating planning and control into a single function and process, but he is still, unfortunately, very rare.

Another strategic decision that must be made to determine the planning approach is between centralized planning and decentralized planning. The Planagement System favors strong guidelines and monitoring by top management, which must have an overview, but leaves to each manager the primary planning and control for his own area of responsibility.

In a speech before a group of professional engineers, an official of a leading oil company revealed that back in 1937 some of the best scientific minds came up with an ambitious technical forecast of scientific breakthroughs that could be expected later in the twentieth century:

> It's interesting to examine this technical forecast today, because it completely overlooked not only the computer, but atomic energy, antibiotics, radar, and jet propulsion. So the next time you hear the experts tell us what to expect in the next 50 years, it might be well to hold some reservations. Things have a way of never turning out as the experts foretell. This is one of the reasons why a wholly-planned society is a stagnant society. The planners are never able to keep abreast of the ingenuity of the human mind.

It would therefore seem wise to include all managers with other than routine responsibility and/or ambition in the planning program.

Table 8. Two basic approaches to planning.

PLAN-ORGANIZE-IMPLEMENT-CONTROL-PLAN	CONTROL-PLAN-ORGANIZE-IMPLEMENT-CONTROL
1. Plan evolves the budget.	1. Budget is established, plan evolved from it.
2. Standard of measurement is potentials.	2. Standard of measurement is past performance.
3. Emphasis is on futures—the unknown.	3. Emphasis is on operations—the known.
4. Definition–analysis–decision–action–control.	4. Sales forecast–profit objective–budget to make happen.
5. Analysis–logic–evolution of standards of performance.	5. Experience–evolution of rules-of-thumb or fixed standards of performance.
6. Marksmanship—draw target, then shoot.	6. Management control—shoot, then draw target.
7. Conceptual qualitative reasoning evolves figures.	7. Pragmatic quantitative reasoning evolves figures.
8. Building-oriented, optimizes.	8. Exploitation-oriented, improves.
9. Emphasizes the mind, logic, plans of action.	9. Emphasizes the budget, numbers control, forecasts.
10. Plan behind the profit.	10. Budget is the profit plan.
11. Long-range bent—futures.	11. Short-range bent—operations.
12. Profitability (imaginative), growth.	12. Profit (measurative), exploit.
13. "Why" is emphasized.	13. "What" is emphasized.
14. Guidelines down—plans and objectives up.	14. Objectives down—agreement-disagreement.
15. Leads to decentralized planning.	15. Leads to centralized planning.
16. Leans toward objective approach.	16. Leans toward subjective approach.
17. Evolves standards—creative, new approach.	17. Defines standards—pragmatic, proven approach.
18. Integrates planning and doing.	18. Tends to separate planning and doing.
19. Responds to present situation and anticipates the future.	19. Responds to history.
20. Leans toward A and B * types of manager and situation.	20. Leans toward C * type of manager and situation.
21. Flexible, dynamic.	21. Fixed, stable.
22. Leans toward anticipating change—better able to stay in tune with changes.	22. Leans toward reacting to change—less able to stay in tune with changes.
23. Pushes through the individual (Theory Y).	23. Pulls from the individual (Theory X).
24. Individual is the primary auditor of his area of responsibility.	24. Centralized control is the auditor.

* The A, B, and C types of manager are discussed in the section on direction in Chapter 14.

Figure 4. Company management, line division, and staff departments. Management guidelines flow down, and plans and exception reports flow up.

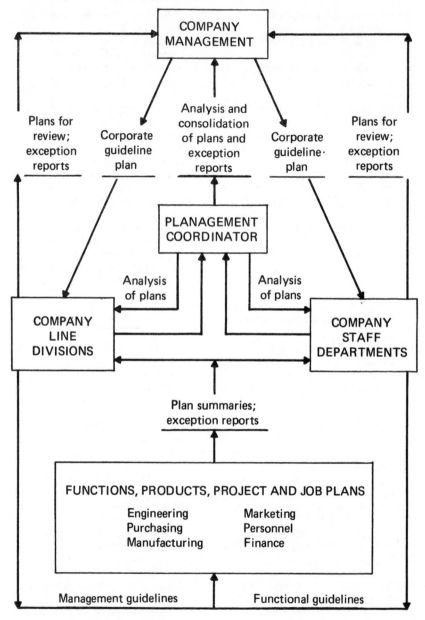

Assuming that decentralized planning and control are adopted, the planning flow in an organization would look like Figure 4.

Strategy Matrix

A good way to establish sound strategy is to develop a strategy matrix of the most important elements in your plan. The matrix will show a number of similar or identical strategies. These are your most important strategies, the ones you will use to identify sound priorities for supporting actions and allocation of resources.

You probably should include at least the following key elements from the written plan you have developed up to now in your strategy matrix:

Most important accountability and mission.

Most important capability and opportunity.

Most important assumption and potential. (Strategies frequently are developed along with assumptions and potentials.)

Most important objectives, including those in the key result areas.

The five most important strategies that are basic to your entire plan.

When you have developed the strategies suggested in this chapter, you will have completed your strategic plan.

Additional items that might be included in the sixth section of your plan are: *policies, procedures,* and *agreements and contracts.* Strategies often generate formal policies, which, in turn, may need the support of step-by-step procedures and written agreements. An example of this would be to take the key result area (employee attitudes and performance) strategy for a twice-a-year performance/development review and make it a written policy in the policy manual. This policy could be supported by a questionnaire (procedure) that would be completed and agreed to by both the employee and his supervisor, and signed by both (contract).

To develop a thorough strategic plan will probably take most of your total planning time. Once the strategic plan is completed, the remaining steps are of a more mechanical operating nature.

10

From Concepts to Reality

THE OPERATING plan is developed in the seventh section of your plan and is composed of the programs, projects, and alternatives you must consider in order to accomplish your plan. These plans of action should operate within the framework of the strategies you established in the preceding chapter (which should be included in Section 6 of your written plan).

How these plans of action are written varies according to need. Regardless of the program or project form selected, certain essential elements of information should be included as part of a sound plan of action. A recommended format, at least for your most important actions and objectives, is Planagement Form PA5B (Figure 5).

This tool should be used only where it will be of assistance. It is important not to spend a dollar's worth of planning for a dime's worth of difference, but it is foolish to attempt to gain a dollar's worth of difference for a dime's worth of planning. Your judgment will determine the depth of the plan, the number of tools used, and how extensively they are used.

Section 6: Policy, Procedures, and Strategy

To return to the salesman's plan, which was developed through Section 5 (objectives) in Chapter 8: The strategy section written in

Figure 5. Planagement form PA5B.

	THIS	REPLACES
FILE:		
DATE:		
PAGE:	OF	OF

PROGRAM SUMMARY

Programs and Projects should be developed for each <u>major</u> action identified throughout the plan.

I. ACTION PROGRAM   Name and number: _____

II. OBJECTIVE (What by When)   Objective number: _____

III. ASSUMPTION/POTENTIAL

IV. STRATEGY (How, Approach)

A. Projects (Action Steps in Sequence)	B. Schedule (When)	C. Responsibility (Who)

V. RESOURCES REQUIRED
   1. Money
   2. Manpower
   3. Materials/Other

VI. COST/BENEFIT PURPOSE/RESULTS (Why)

VII. ALTERNATIVES CONSIDERED (Description and Disposition)

Section 6 will provide the framework for the operating plan in Section 7.

Salesman's Plan—Section 6

The primary *policy* in this plan is that the customer-first philosophy will be followed; he will be considered right until an investigation in accordance with Procedure No. 21 in the *Procedures Manual* determines that he is in error. An additional policy is that no customer is to be contacted directly by anyone in the company until he first clears it with the salesman responsible for the account. The *strategies* most important to this plan are:

* Adoption of a key account program.
* Use of a direct mail campaign to supplement my personal sales effort.
* Offsetting of the negative economic environment and the slowdown in the growth of the market by increasing market penetration at a more rapid rate.
* Communication of market needs and competitive product developments to the company's research and development manager.
* Development of a written career plan, including a management/self-development program, applying the same Planagement System that was used to develop this plan.

The strategy in support of my *most important accountability,* which is to increase volume of sales, is the key account program.

The strategy in support of my *personal mission* is to develop a formal, written career plan and a personal development program.

The strategy in support of my *most important capability* and *opportunity* is to increase market penetration at a more rapid rate through the creation and use of a key account program.

The strategy in support of the *most important assumption* in this plan is to keep the R&D department informed of market needs and competitive product changes.

For the *most important potential,* the strategy is to increase market penetration through a key account program.

The strategy in support of my *most important objective* is to earn a promotion because of superior performance, which should be achieved through the key account program and the personal self-improvement that is fostered by my formal written career and self-development plan.

With this strategy matrix approach, the most important strategies become more apparent because they are repeated more frequently than others. The frequency of repetition throughout the plan is a frustration to many who have applied the Planagement process—myself included. But the repetition, by identifying the most important elements in the plan in their proper order of importance, accomplishes the main goal of planning—which is to establish the most important objectives in order of priority and then allocate the available resources accordingly. In our example, the salesman's most important strategies revolve around his key account and personal development programs, indicating that these are the first two plans of action he should develop.

Section 7: Programs, Projects, and Alternatives

It is suggested that you now review your own plan, particularly the strategy matrix, to see if the most important programs, in order of priority, are readily identifiable. These programs should be listed in the seventh section of your plan and supported by completed program/project sheets.

Salesman's Plan—Section 7

The most important *programs* in order of their importance are: the key account program; the self-development program and written career plan; the written report to the research and development department; and the direct mail campaign. The completed key account program summary is shown in Figure 6.

It is interesting to note that frequently when the program sheet is completed, the objective and/or its date are revised. The reason is that the objective is now more thoroughly planned and hence easier to accomplish.

Once the operating plans are complete, the remaining sections of the Planagement Plan are a summary of the resources required to accomplish the plan. These resources, or assets to be employed, are people, money, materials, time, and space.

Section 8: Priorities and Schedules

The time required to implement the plan is summarized in an operational schedule listing objectives, supporting programs, projects, and key milestones in their order of priority. This operational

Figure 6. Key account program summary (Form PA5B).

	THIS	REPLACES
FILE:	7A1	
DATE:	1/10/XX	
PAGE:	1 OF 1	OF

PROGRAM SUMMARY

Programs and projects should be
developed for each major action
identified throughout the plan.

I. ACTION PROGRAM   Name and number: Key Account Program
Program 7A1

II. OBJECTIVE (What by When)   Objective number: 5B1

To use my time more effectively through the establishment of a key
account program by 7/31/xx, and to increase market penetration at a
more rapid rate.

III. ASSUMPTION/POTENTIAL

A. It is assumed that 20% of the customers account for 80% of the
potential.

B. 85% of the market with an estimated value of $8,500,000 is not
served by our products.

IV. STRATEGY (How, Approach)

Identify the key accounts that comprise 80% of the potential and
rank them according to magnitude of potential.

A. Projects (Action Steps in Sequence)	B. Schedule (When)	C. Responsibility (Who)
1. Get approval of this plan.	1. 2/10/xx	1. Mine, plus my boss's.
2. Identify and rank the most important customers who qualify as key accounts, based on a potential of at least $100,000.	2. 5/10/xx	2. Mine, with help from R & D.
3. Establish a schedule for calls based on the rank established.	3. 6/15/xx	3. Mine.
4. Implement the key account program.	4. 7/1/xx	4. Mine.
5. Measure progress and report it.	5. 7/31/xx	5. Mine, with review by my boss.

Figure 6 (cont.)

V. RESOURCES REQUIRED

1. Money—within my established budget.
2. Manpower—20% of my time; eventually, 80% of my selling time or about 65% of my total time.
3. Materials/Others—Key account list for calls.

VI. COST/BENEFIT PURPOSE/RESULTS (Why)

The cost is within budget and will require up to 65% of my time. The benefits will be increased sales volume due to increased market penetration, and more effective and efficient use of my time.

VII. ALTERNATIVES CONSIDERED (Description and Disposition)

A. Increase sales with present customers.
B. Concentrate on customers closest to my office in order to reduce the travel time required.

schedule (Form PA6), which is shown in Figure 7, provides an excellent overview of the plan and is a good monitoring device.

Section 9: Organization, Delegation, and Development

Assuming you have completed the written operational schedule for your own plan, the next step is to add up the human resources that are required to accomplish your plan. The ninth section of your plan includes such factors as organization, delegation, and development. If an organization change is required, or if more people are needed, here is where you indicate it. Here is also where you include your self-development program, which is based on any deficiencies you have discovered in yourself vis-à-vis your present job and the job you are working toward.

This is a crucially important section because your plan, or any plan, is only as sound as the people who created it and have the responsibility for making it an operating reality. In today's age of rapid change, a person is either growing or becoming obsolete; there is no middle ground. What is and is not included in Section 9 of an in-

Figure 7. Salesman's plan—Section 8 (Form PA6).

OPERATIONAL SCHEDULE Priorities/Schedules

ORIGINATOR:
DISTRIBUTION:
SUBJECT: Objectives/Programs/Projects/Key Milestones

	THIS	REPLACES
FILE:	0.8	
DATE:	1/10/XX	
PAGE:	1 OF 1	0*

Objectives and/or Projects	Number	Jan.	Feb.	Mar.	2Qtr.	3Qtr.	4Qtr.	19xx + 1 1	2	19xx + 2	19xx + 3	19xx + 4	19xx + 5
Year →								**UNITS OF TIME**					
1 To earn a promotion	5F & C1						→			12/31			
2 Key account program	5B					→ 7/31							
3 Approval of plan	1		→10										
4 Identification of key accounts	2				→ 5/10								
5 Schedule of calls	3				→ 6/15								
6 Implementation	4					→ 7/1							
7 Measure progress and report	5					→ 7/31							
8 Sales forecast	5A1						12/31	→ 12/31	12/31				
9 Self-development program	5A3						→ 10/1	Each quarter continuously					
10 New report to R & D	5A2				→ 6/1								
11													

dividual's Planagement Plan frequently provides a good insight into whether he is growing or becoming obsolete. By the same token, what is included in Section 9 by a company and key organizational units will identify in which direction the organization is moving.

Assuming you have completed the ninth section of your own written plan, how would you appraise our salesman? Is he moving toward growth or obsolescence? Now, how would you appraise your own direction? Have you written the answers to these questions:

- Is an organizational change required to accomplish your plan?
- If so, what is it?
- Do you require additional people? What kind? How many?
- Do you have a career plan in writing?
- Do you have a written self-development program?

Salesman's Plan—Section 9

The accomplishment of my plan does not require any *organizational changes now*. However, if I increase my market penetration to 30 percent of the market, a *back-up man* will be needed.

I intend to use the Planagement System to develop a career plan in writing by the end of this year, and it will include my Objective 5A3, which is part of my *self-development program*, and requires my attending at least one management development program each year and completing at least one book or home study course on management each quarter, starting October 1, 19xx.

I will measure the success of this self-development program by how well I implement my plan and by whether or not I accomplish my most important objective, which is to earn a promotion to district manager by December 31, 19xx + 3. It is interesting to note that if I meet or surpass my forecast, my office will have achieved by December 31, 19xx + 2 a sales level and market penetration that exceeds that of one-third of the company's district offices, and could well be made into a district office with the assignment of a back-up man. This change would give me a management- as well as sales-oriented job.

Section 10: Budgets and Resources

Questions you should answer in writing this section of your plan include:

- What is your operating budget?
- What is your cash flow of income over expenditures or other allocations of cash?

- What additional capital do you require over and above your budget and cash flow, and when will this capital be required?
- What does your short-term and long-term balance sheet (assuming one is needed) look like—is it reduced to writing?
- What gaps exist between management guidelines and your plan, or between what is wanted and what is achievable?
- What additional resources do you require to accomplish your plan? When are they required?

Salesman's Plan—Section 10

The *operating budget* is figured at 20 percent of the forecasted sales volume. It amounts to $36,000, and is sufficient to accomplish this plan.

Sales generated will amount to $180,000 in 19xx, and $570,000 over the next three years, of which 80 percent (or $456,000) will be *cash flow* generated to the company through sales volume, less my operating budget.

If we are converted into a district office because of the sales volume generated in 19xx + 2, we will probably be assigned a back-up man; however, this addition to the budget should not require *additional capital* because the sales forecast will be increased due to the success of the key account program. Thus the key operating ratio of budget to sales volume should be maintained, and possibly improved, even though a back-up man is added to the staff.

A *balance sheet* is not required in this plan because the company is the only entity that can measure liabilities and thus define the equity position.

There is no *gap* in this plan because the plan exceeds the guidelines provided by management.

The additional major *resources* required to accomplish the plan are: a key account plan; a career plan and self-development program; a new report to research and development; a back-up man by December 31, 19xx + 2; an opportunity for promotion; up to 65 percent of my time for the key account plan.

Section 11: Justifications, Results, and Profitability

In this final section of your plan, you should write down your answers to at least these questions:

- What are the most important justifications for approving your plan—the primary results to be achieved from accomplishing this plan?

- What are the gains from each of the major objectives and supporting programs as determined by a cost/benefit analysis?
- What key recommendations do you have, and what is their justification for approval?
- How do you measure the key gains, including reason sheets, payouts, cost-saving statements, quantified results, qualitative gains list, and other statements that identify the gain to be derived from accomplishing the plan?

The eleventh section of your plan records the overall gains to be achieved. It identifies why you want to, and why you should, accomplish the plan you have submitted (the sixth step of the logic process).

After you have completed this section of your own written plan, ask yourself if you would approve the plan if it was submitted to you. If so, why?

On the basis of your review of the eleventh section of the salesman's plan, together with the preceding sections, would you approve his plan? If so, why? How do you know it is sound? How do you know your own plan is sound?

Salesman's Plan—Section 11

The most important *justifications* include increased sales volume, increased market penetration, and a stronger person who could be considered for promotion to district manager within the next three years.

It is recommended that this office be made a district office by December 31, 19xx + 2 if the forecast is achieved, because its sales volume will then exceed that of at least one-third of all the other offices, and there should be a district manager in charge of this volume with a back-up man to insure it is maintained, increased, and protected.

Preparing for Leadership

If you were this salesman's supervisor, by reading his plan you would gain a good insight into his thinking, judgment, and potential. You would be able to estimate his future contributions and judge his requirements for improving his productivity.

By applying the Planagement method to his job, the salesman is viewing his job as a business and is thinking like a general manager charged with the responsibility of controlling and improving the gain (results) from his activity. This view and posture will contribute to his growth and development, and will help him to more effectively manage himself, his job, his accounts, his territory's potential, and eventually the responsibilities of a district, regional, and sales manager—perhaps even a general manager, since that is the role he is performing in regard to his present sales job.

Don't forget that your guideline plan, as represented in Sections 1 through 11, is not an end but rather a beginning to a highly productive, exceptionally rewarding, continual process. It is, in fact, a way of life that should result in your joining that elite group who are the leaders in their chosen fields.

Without question, the price is almost as high as the rewards. Whether or not you accomplish your plan depends on you and how much self-discipline you use in support of your plan. This self-discipline is demonstrated in part by your taking the required actions in accordance with the priorities and time schedule you established in Section 8. In addition, you will need the self-discipline to manage changes affecting your plan, including those you did not anticipate. There will be times when you will need to change your plan by using the unique Planagement Exception Report, which is reviewed in the next chapter.

II

Establishing a Living Plan

WHILE PLANS are useful, it is the planning process that is indispensable. Sections 1 through 11 of the Planagement System provide a format and guide for identifying, gathering, organizing, analyzing, and presenting the minimum amount of information required for planning, decision making, and control. Section 12 of the Planagement System introduces the unique Planagement tool—the *exception report*—whose primary purpose is to create a constantly current living plan.

Section 12: The Exception Report

One of the biggest challenges facing the Planager is that of balancing the responsibility for accomplishing the established plan with the need to keep the plan dynamic and in tune with changes that have an impact on it. It is critically important to keep the plan up-to-date on a continuous basis. In order to reduce paperwork and the time spent on the mechanics of planning to an absolute minimum, managing and reporting by exception were made a basic part of the Planagement process. It is the exception reporting that makes the Planagement System a closed-loop process that constantly reinforces and improves itself.

Because of a variety of mental filters and other human hang-ups, the average person must be repeatedly exposed to a piece of

103

Figure 8. Exception report (Form PA7).

EXCEPTION REPORT

Originator: ...(Salesman's name)...   Area: ...(Territory name)...   Date: ...2/10/xx...

Distribution: ...(Supervisor's name)...   File: ...12.1...

Copies (Others Affected): Manager of R & D Department

Reference: REVISED EXECUTIVE SUMMARY SECTION(S) ATTACHED AS CIRCLED (1) .2 .3 (4) .5 .6 .7 .8 .9 .10 (11)

REFERENCE (OBJECTIVE NO., FUNCTION OR PRODUCT PLAN NAME):

My job plan (Reference Coordination Report 4C1)

I. NATURE OF CHANGE(S) AND CAUSE FOR THE CHANGE(S) PRESENT AND/OR ANTICIPATED: 1. NATURE OF BUSINESS/ FUNCTION. 2. ENVIRONMENT/COMPETITION. 3. CAPABILITIES/OPPORTUNITIES. 4. ASSUMPTIONS/POTENTIALS.

Company's R & D department advises that each 1% of the market I serve is worth $120,000, rather than my estimated $100,000, which is an increase of 20%.

II. MAJOR NEEDS, PROBLEMS, ADVANTAGES, OPPORTUNITIES CAUSED BY CHANGE (PRESENT AND/OR ANTICIPATED).

III. ADJUSTMENTS TO BE MADE AND RESULTS EXPECTED: 5. OBJECTIVES/GOALS. 6. POLICIES/PROCEDURES/STRATEGY. 7. PROGRAMS/PROJECTS/ALTERNATIVES. 8. PRIORITIES/SCHEDULES. 9. ORGANIZATION/DELEGATION/DEVELOPMENT. 10. BUDGETS/RESOURCES. 11. JUSTIFICATION(S).

The potential and forecast will have to be revised, as well as the estimated market penetration in Section 1. Replace the pages that are no longer valid in Sections 1, 4, 5, and 11 with the updated pages attached to this report.

IV. IMPACT OF CHANGE ON OBJECTIVE(S)—I.E., FORECAST/ACTUAL. 5. RESTATEMENT OF OBJECTIVE(S):

The forecast and results will be increased by 10% and the market share and potential will be revised.

Approved by .... Date ....

V. SUMMARY. (CHECK ONE AND INCLUDE COMMENTS AND/OR ATTACHMENTS AS REQUIRED.)

A. ☐ Off Plan (See above and required attachment(s).)

B. ☐ On Plan (No change(s); this form complete if this box is checked.)

C. ☒ Plan Changed

Submitted by .... (Name of salesman)
....
Position .... (Salesman—XX territory)............

knowledge before that knowledge is stored forever in his brain as an available resource. In order to report by exception, the manager must review his plan and the changes that have occurred or are anticipated, and this constant review instills the plan in his mind. Also, the constant reporting of exceptions establishes a habit of managing change to advantage. It overcomes the common pitfall of letting planning become a once-a-year exercise, with plans put on the shelf and forgotten—or kept apart from operations.

The exception report and feedback system have other advantages and strengths. For example, man is basically a goal-oriented being. Once he sets a clear goal or objective in his mind, he virtually *must* accomplish that goal, and he will not be satisfied until he does. In the Planagement process a goal or objective clearly emerges, and through the exception-reporting process becomes—along with the entire plan—a part of the person's mind. He must, therefore, accomplish his plan. And he is armed with a powerful tool that establishes a habit for managing change, staying on target, and controlling the desired results.

No one can motivate someone else. One person may stimulate or excite another, but a stimulus is only temporary. Real motivation is a long-lasting, internal self-discipline that causes someone to strive toward an objective because he believes in it. Once a motive is clearly and consciously established, the person will be committed to taking action to support it. The basic idea of the Planagement System is to provide you with the tool you need to take advantage of your innate mental capacities and acquire the self-discipline to become a constantly growing person.

Another benefit of the exception report is that you will become your own auditor. You will begin to realize that there are no scapegoats or excuses for failure, that you are responsible for the realization of your own potential. No longer will you feel dependent on circumstances for your personal success, because you will be one of those rare persons who clearly understands that "if everyone would sweep his own front porch, the whole city would be clean."

Exception Report Form PA7 is the basis for Section 12 of the Planagement System. Using this form (Figure 8), write down any changes that have occurred or are anticipated. Next, record how you will manage these changes and what impact those managed changes will have on your plan and its expected results. If the plan needs to be changed, attach the updated pages to the exception report. When the exception report is approved, incorporate the current pages into the plan and remove the obsolete pages. You will then have a living plan—usually, an improved plan.

There are additional reasons for using the management-by-exception concept, and one of the most important involves a characteristic of the human mind. Modern psychology (and ancient wisdom) tells us that people feel and act in accordance with what they *imagine* to be true about themselves and their environment. By documenting a complete plan, you will gain a more objective insight into the facts and judgment you used to establish the plan and you will be able to identify errors at the very beginning. Then the exception-reporting procedure will require you to reevaluate objectively your original views in the light of experience, new knowledge, and changes.

Communication by Exception

In order to be able to communicate by exception, we must have a standard or base against which exceptions can be identified and measured. A picture of the concept of communicating by exception might be constructed as follows. We start off with where we are now, based on identification and analysis of the facts as we think they are (Steps 1 and 2 of the Planagement-logic process). Next we make our best assumption (guesstimate) as to what the future will look like (Step 3 of the Planagement process) and establish an objective (Step 4). Then we determine how and when we are going to accomplish the objective, who will be responsible for what actions, and how much we are willing to pay (Step 5). Finally, we justify why we are moving in the direction we established (Step 6) and identify changes in the original situation and manage these exceptions (exception reporting—Step 7).

Our complete picture looks like Figure 9, in which the plan is the standard, and changes are depicted as *A, B,* and *C.* Notice how

Figure 9. The dynamic communication-by-exception process.

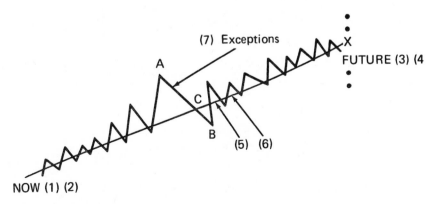

the impact of change is reduced from A to B to A to C and C to B until the change is not so great and is more easily managed. Because we have a plan, we have a base for quickly identifying exceptions (change), and because we know the direction and magnitude of the change, we can make the *proper* corrections and keep our objectives in tune with the changes—bad or good.

The overall result of establishing a plan is that you will become anticipative rather than responsive, a problem preventer rather than a problem solver. You will be more effective and efficient because you will do the right things the right way the first time around. Once you can do more in less time with better results, you will be able to more favorably influence your environment and future.

Part IV

How to Successfully Implement the System

12

A Plan for Management

An individual or organization that does not plan
and manage the future may not have one.

How DO YOU implement the Planagement program? Unfortunately, there is no one answer to this question because the method of implementation varies according to the particular situation. One situation is rarely the same as another because people are unique and businesses differ.

This fact was made abundantly clear when the Planagement System was taught to a group of senior executives in a program sponsored by a highly respected university. The 36 participants were introduced to the Planagement System and then asked to review the example plan that the application of the Planagement System had produced. They were requested to divide themselves into three groups of 12 each. Each group was given the same enumerated exceptions and asked to update the plan with an exception report. All three groups brought back a different plan, and each one strongly defended its plan as the best.

Several important insights came out of this experience. First, there is no perfect plan or one best plan. Plans are created by people, and people are different, so the plans they create will be different. (The same is true for teams.) Second, a person will be very committed to a plan if he, or his team, created it. A good plan wholeheartedly supported by its managers has a better chance of succeeding than an excellent plan whose managers are unenthusiastic. Third, while the Planagement program could and should remain consistent, its implementation has to be tailored to the people, the organization, and the nature of the business if it is going to work to best advantage. In other words, the plan for implementing the planning program should be created by those responsible for the implementation of the program; the planner and the doer should be one and the same. This being said, we can turn to the basic principles and approaches evolved from a wide application of the program in a variety of situations.

Introduction of the Planagement System

Generally, the best place to start the program is at the top, with the chief executive officer, the chief operating officer, and the managers who report directly to these officers. Planning is hard work, and unless top management sets the example, it is unlikely that other managers will take the planning effort very seriously. In most companies it is the president who determines the climate, and the proper internal environment will greatly facilitate the program's reception. It is also desirable that guidelines be issued from the top so that everyone understands the desired direction and acts in support of it.

After the initial planning efforts are completed by the top management team, a guideline plan should be constructed. Ideally, the president would then write a personal letter to his managers announcing his intention to turn the company around from an average profit performer to a dynamic, growing enterprise. He would introduce the system by stating its basic purposes: "to create a design for the company's future that is in the best interests of all who depend upon it—management, employees, stockholders, customers, and society—and to provide for the systematic rational use of resources that will assist us to make that future a reality." In further explication he might write:

. The concept behind the system is disarmingly simple. Essentially, it is just a matter of determining where we are, where we want to go, and how we can get there. It is not so simple to apply such a theory to a large and complex organization, but the discipline of corporate planning, which has been emerging over the past several years, affords the techniques needed to turn theory into effective practice.

For many months the inside directors have been working diligently with our corporate planning staff on the task of defining our company's basic objectives and priorities. We have attempted to draw a blueprint projecting the company's next three years—insofar as possible—as the basis for the supporting plans to be formulated by each division, major operating unit, and principal staff function.

A basic objective of our Planagement System is to transfer the maximum feasible responsibility, with commensurate authority, to divisional management and all other levels of management. Wherever feasible, each of you will develop your own management plan (which is implicit in your job description), showing specific responsibility for your own section of the corporate plan and the actions you intend to take to implement it.

We are moving toward the day when, with plans established and documented, we will be able to concentrate on opportunities, problems, and changes that deviate significantly from plan and to quickly take the responsive action needed to reach our common objectives. This so-called management by exception, we are convinced, offers us the kind of control of our enterprise that is now demanded for consistent success and progress.

Our Corporate Strategic Guideline Plan represents a major milestone in our company's history and the foundation stone for a new thrust in company management philosophy. This is not because the plan embodies any unique concepts, but rather because it is the essential first step toward a more rational, practical, and workable management system—one that will actually put all the talent and initiative of our excellent management team to full use and direct its power toward important and well-defined goals.

There is, in fact, nothing "finished" or sacred about the plan. It merely represents the clearest expression we have been able to make of the path to be taken for the company's immediate future. The supporting plans, which you will formulate at divisional and other levels, will progressively sharpen and clarify the Corporate Strategic Plan. That is one of the real strengths of the Planagement System. It is not imposed from the top down, but only guided. It calls for your *participation* rather than your conformance.

This type of introduction is not just reserved to large corporations. One of the best ways to introduce the planning program is illustrated by the following speech, which was made by a president of a smaller corporation to the thirty managers who comprised his entire management team. The title of his address was "Why We Must Plan."

The question of "why we must plan" is a valid one and should be discussed. Planning requires a great deal of time, and often the benefits and results are difficult to clearly measure.

In addition, none of us really likes to plan. It is a self-discipline that we prefer to avoid. Psychologists have discovered through research that there are three things people don't like: they don't like to think; they don't like paperwork; and they don't like to use orderly procedures.

Speaking for myself, I can assure each of you that the psychologists are right. I don't like to do these three things, but since they constitute the basic self-discipline of planning, I know I must do them successfully to meet my responsibilities as a manager.

The purpose of my following remarks is to share with you some insights I have gained concerning the subject of planning that have made it easier for me to do it. In fact, I now find that planning makes my work easier and much more satisfying.

The first insight concerns the basic elements of our job as managers. It doesn't matter whether we hold the position responsibility of president, sales manager, or first-line supervisor; we all share the responsibility inherent in being a manager, and only the magnitude differs. As managers, we must plan, organize, implement, and control. These four responsibilities are obvious—we all know them. The interesting aspect is that three of the four (planning, organizing, and controlling) are planning in nature and requirement. In other words, 75 percent of our management skill depends on our planning skill. This makes it pretty clear that planning is every manager's job—in fact, it is most of his job, and to delegate this role to someone else is to stop being a productive manager.

Actually, all of us plan and have been doing so since we were able to think for ourselves. Planning really is applied common sense, but as Emerson observed, "The trouble with common sense is that it is too uncommon." I'm sure you would agree with me that too often this is the case. Part of the reason is our unwillingness to apply the self-discipline required to accomplish planning. But even more than that, most people do not understand what planning is and how it works and why it works as it does. The task, then, is one of understanding planning and teaching it to others.

I'm sure all of us are well aware of the many benefits to be gained from successfully implementing a sound planning effort. Two of the more important benefits are:

1. Being able to do more in less time with better results. In other words, it will make our jobs easier.

2. It would also mean greater profits and growth for us, as individuals and as a corporation.

As a matter of fact, research has shown that corporations that earn over a 10 percent return on investment after taxes—the elite of American industry—have only one thing in common: their top managers spend over 50 percent of their time planning.

You know, another interesting fact about this admittedly nebulous subject of planning is that the average human being uses only 5 percent of his mental capacity. As managers, because of the skills we must develop and employ, we use between 10 and 13 percent of our mental ability (Einstein, one of our greatest thinkers, used only 22 percent). Without question, our greatest potential as individuals, and collectively as a corporation, lies in mastering the ability to work smarter, not just harder. Planning is the mental discipline and conscious application of common sense that allows each one of us to do more of the *right things* as well as *doing things right*. That is the real distinction between being effective and being merely efficient. The successful application of a sound planning process is the basic difference between a good company and a great company. It is the difference between being the leader in an industry and being a follower. The constant application of the fundamentals of sound, conscious thinking will determine the kind of future we will have as individuals and as a corporation.

I am committed to using a planning process that has been developed by several hundred operating managers who recognized the need to turn the theory of planning into a practical and productive management tool. This tool, called Planagement, makes it much easier for us to develop a system to successfully manage change so that we become problem preventers, not just problem solvers. The tool that I refer to has structured the skill of planning in such a way that it can easily be practiced by each of us. In addition, we will be able to teach this skill to those who work with us.

I'm really very pleased to be able to introduce to you this newly developed Planagement method for planning and management. It will, I'm convinced, make our jobs a lot easier and more rewarding. Through the use of this tool, we will be better able to consistently manage inconsistent situations in a way that will produce constant gain. Through our own more rapid growth as people, we will continue to build our corporation as a recognized leader both nationally and internationally.

Management at the corporate offices has already used the Planagement System, and we will develop our Corporate Guideline Plan in the very near future. Much of this plan will include the fine plans you have already developed. Obviously, we have to take a broader and longer look at the situation. Over the next few months we will all participate in formulating our company's strategic view.

How important is this to us? A recent study indicates that the soundness of corporate strategy determines at least 70 percent of a corporation's future success. That is why we must plan.

I'm confident that each of you will welcome, support, and actively participate in the successful implementation of our planning program. I can promise you that through the use of this applied common-sense approach for planning and managing we will be able to realize the corporation's exceptional potential for profits, growth, and personal satisfaction.

This, of course, is just an example. The method of introduction should be tailored to the personality, style, and preference of the president, and the needs and structure of the organization.

Criteria for the Planagement Program

One of the guidelines for implementation is to decide what you specifically want to accomplish with your planning/management/control program. This should assist you to select the right program and approach.

The most important criteria usually desired by management are that the program

Be simple, yet practical.
Be selective in nature.
Be universally applicable.
Be firm, with balanced flexibility.
Provide essentials and be precise.
Reflect change through feedback via exception reporting.
Lend itself to computerizing feedback and adjustment.
Integrate individual goals with corporate goals.
Be problem-preventing in nature.
Develop the individual.
Provide objective standards for measuring performance and awarding compensation.
Stimulate management support.
Minimize paperwork.
Provide methodology to produce desired results.
Balance freedom with discipline.
Use the logic process to evolve sound objectives.
Be a management tool for a common language, format, and approach.

More particular results frequently requested by managers are to:

"Increase profits, accelerate growth, establish sound diversification."
"Double return on investment."
"Help to create new product—faster commercialization."
"Reduce paperwork—fewer staff meetings."
"Improve growth and development of managers."
"Improve communications and understanding."
"Change functional thinking to profit and growth thinking."
"Give more realistic and accurate forecasting."
"Establish simple feedback and update method."
"Result in participative management and increased delegation—make promotion from within a viable practice."
"Move toward a total management information system; bridge gap between people and computers."
"Stimulate the entrepreneur in people."
"Refresh the skills of senior managers, strengthen the skills of middle managers, and teach skills to new managers."

These criteria provide the specifications for the planning/management program to meet and also establish a base for measuring the performance and results of the program. Unless the results wanted are clearly identified, it will be difficult, if not impossible, to create a tailored program and objectively measure its performance.

Initial Plan and Approach of the Planagement Program

Once the results you wish to achieve are clearly spelled out in writing, the next step involves some tough decisions about how the results are to be achieved. Ask yourself the following questions:

Planning manager or coordinator?
Central or individual planning?
Formal or informal planning?
What planning cycle?
Operational versus strategic versus tactical?
Who will participate?
How will planning program be implemented?
What planning format is best?
What is minimum information needed for sound decisions?
Sell or tell? Guide or direct? Procedure or judgment?
Should information be held confidential?
How often should plan be reviewed?
How much time for planning?
Any outside help?
What degree of individual freedom?
How should we measure planning activity?
What is acceptable for the plan?
What basic approaches should be taken?

The question pertaining to outside help is a very important one. There are significant arguments on both sides of this question, but probably the best answer is not a commitment to either an outside resource or an inside person, but rather a combination of both. In any case, it is of vital importance that an in-house Planagement capability be established for the reasons previously discussed.

Still, it is wise to consider using a licensed Planagement counselor in the initial stages of your program for these reasons:

1. Because he is trained in the Planagement skill, he will save you and your management team time, and this savings in time should more than pay for his services. He will be able to help you

tailor the program to your unique requirements and still maintain the integrity of the Planagement discipline.

2. His past experience will enable him to present some profitable ideas, alternatives, and sound strategies for your consideration.

3. He will provide the initially needed self-discipline, objective viewpoint, expert documentation, and attention to detail, as well as an independent critique of the plan created.

4. Your people will usually relate more openly to an outsider who is a professional in his field.

5. The Planagement counselor will have access to other specialists who can, if necessary, be utilized in support of your planning effort. Because they are trained in the Planagement skill, they can do more, in less time, with better results. It will be easy to coordinate and consolidate their work with your plans because they will have developed their information in the same Planagement format.

6. Since the Planagement counselor keeps up-to-date on new and improved approaches, products, and developments, you will be assured of a constantly current program.

7. He has access to a great deal of data, resource material, examples, teaching devices, programs, and supporting personnel in many locations—all of which are usually beyond the scope of an organization.

8. He has met the rigorous standards required of an authorized Planagement counselor; you are, therefore, assured the services of a professional who has the total support of the organization he represents. He will accomplish the agreed-on results prior to submitting his invoice.

9. The Planagement counselor is teaching-oriented and can effectively conduct in-house training and development seminars. In addition, he will teach a person from either within or outside your organization to be your in-house Planagement practitioner, thereby eliminating himself.

When considering the basic approach to be taken to your planning program, it is suggested that you employ the self-reinforcing Planagement implementation process:

Response: Evolve a tailored plan for planning, including criteria and results.

Definition: Establish the approved plan for planning in writing, using the Planagement approach and tools.

Implementation: Make the plan for planning happen.

Evaluation: Identify the results of the Planagement planning program and the plan for planning against the original criteria, and document exceptions in exception reports.

Response: Convert and improve the plan for planning as indicated by the exception reports.*

An example of this type of plan for implementing the Planagement program is included in the appendix.

Who Should Be Included, and How Will the Plan Be Implemented?

Who will be included in the Planagement program and how the program will be implemented to improve organizational communications, coordination, cooperation, and consolidation of plans are very important initial decisions. The implementation should be carried out so that team planning will evolve into individual planning for jobs and careers, because unless the Planagement program is used individually as well as collectively, the maximum benefits will probably not be obtained.

As a general guideline, it is suggested that the Planagement program include everyone with other than routine responsibility and ambition. The only criterion for participation should be a desire to improve oneself, one's performance, and one's present situation, and a commitment to acquire and apply the self-discipline necessary to do this. The program should include all managers from the president to the first-line supervisor in the plant. Salesmen in the field and secretaries should also be included. The latter are usually one of the most underutilized resources in a company; properly used, they can free up to 50 percent of the manager's time, and thus will have a major impact on improving present management productivity. In addition, they will provide an expanded pool of potential managers and administrative assistants. As previously stated, however, implementation should begin at the top in order to communicate the organization's direction so that lower-level managers can construct appropriate supporting plans.

The initial guideline plan can usually be created in two days by the top management team with the aid of a Planagement counselor. The results are:

The Planagement skill will be transferred to participants.
A summary guideline plan will be developed.
The Planagement counselor will document the plan.
A plan for tailoring and implementing the Planagement System will be developed.

* Copyright © 1974, Planagement, Inc.

A president or other senior manager, working alone with a Planagement counselor, can probably write a guideline plan in one day and achieve the same basic results. But since his team will not have participated in the development of the guideline, it will not have been trained in Planagement.

An alternative approach is an implementation program that usually takes five days and involves up to eight key managers. The first two days would be spent on individual interviews (approximately two hours each) and a review of the organization's planning. On the third day the Planagement counselor would consolidate and document the information he has received, introduce the Planagement presentation, and give his consolidation report to the managers. The fourth and fifth days would be devoted to management team application. The results of this approach are:

Each manager will learn Planagement skill through participation and application.

A consolidated guideline plan will be developed and documented by the Planagement counselor.

The company's major strengths, problems, potentials, and objectives will be identified and documented by the Planagement counselor.

The management team will have applied the Planagement tool together.

The management team will define and develop the organization's guideline plan and supporting action plans.

The guideline plan will be documented by the Planagement counselor, who will also give recommendations for successfully tailoring and implementing the program in order to obtain the maximum results.

Several benefits exist in this type of implementation. It gives an excellent insight into which of the managers reporting to the president might make a good back-up. It allows everyone an independent say as to what the guideline plan should be. (This opportunity usually generates a number of good ideas that might not emerge if the president were the dominating influence.) The consolidation will make areas of agreement and disagreement and key gaps and needs readily discernible, as well as identify some new or previously unrecognized opportunities. A more thorough and comprehensive guideline plan will usually be created in the two-day team application.

Still another implementation approach would be to have a

group of managers attend a one-day or half-day application workshop where the Planagement System would be introduced and they would be asked to prove its value through their own application. The workshop would also generate the individual plans needed to support the guideline plans created for the company's divisions, departments, functions, and other units. The Planagement counselor would obtain enough feedback from the managers to be able to tailor the program to their needs. The results of this type of application are:

The Planagement concept and method will be introduced.

The Planagement skill will be applied in a workshop by each participant, who will therefore be able to evolve a written individual plan.

The Planagement counselor will make recommendations for tailoring and implementing the Planagement method to obtain the best results.

There are many other ways in which the Planagement program can be implemented; however, the above approaches have proved to be very effective in a wide variety of companies and situations.

The most common approach to implementing a Planagement program is illustrated in Figure 10 and supported by ten sequenced steps:

1. The president and the five managers reporting to him create the company's guideline plan.
2. Each of the five managers meets with the managers reporting to him to create a supporting plan.
3. The supporting plans are reviewed and approved.
4. The supporting plans are consolidated into a company supporting plan.
5. The consolidated supporting plan is compared to the original guideline plan, and existing gaps or needed changes are reviewed and approved. The updated and approved guideline plan and supporting plan are issued to each of the managers who report to the president. They then have the responsibility for implementing their own supporting plans according to the revised company guideline plan and supporting plan.
6. Supporting plans are revised by exception report, if necessary, to conform to the company guideline and supporting plans.

Figure 10. Approach to implementing Planagement program in an organization.

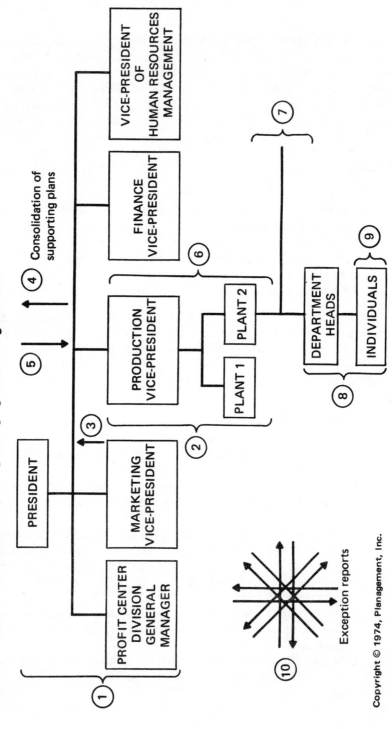

7. The supporting managers to the five vice-presidents would each meet with their team, develop a supporting plan, and submit it for approval. Once each plan is approved, it becomes the guideline plan for the next level.
8. The department heads create their plans supporting the guideline plan of their manager.
9. Individuals reporting to a department head develop their own written plans for their jobs and futures.
10. Exception reporting keeps the plans current and living. If a Planagement coordinator is used to implement the Planagement program and consolidate exception reports for the company, the functioning Planagement implementation system would look like Figure 11.

In this approach, the coordination report was mentioned. The purpose of the coordination report is to document assumed support from others and to make sure that they have a clear understanding of what is needed, by when, and why. They will include this information in their own Planagement plans and agree to report by exception to whomever they are supporting.

The coordination report (Planagement Form PA3—see Figure 12) is the tool that makes it possible to review and improve the informal organization that exists in every dynamic company. It will contribute to changing functional thinking into profit thinking, and it will allow increased delegation and improved communication.

Policy and Communications

Assuming that the plan for implementing the Planagement program has been approved, the next and final step would be to make the program a matter of company policy. Statements of policy may be simple. For example:

> Everyone with other than routine responsibility and ambition will develop a written plan for his job and the goals he desires to achieve. After his plan has been approved by his immediate supervisor, he will keep it current with exception reports made at least once a month.

A flow chart of communications (Figure 13) might be issued to establish the coordination report as a working tool in the organization. *Vertical* communication and coordination flow between the levels of management, regardless of the number of levels. *Lateral*

Figure 11. Flow of management guidelines down and plans and exception reports up and laterally: Company management, line division, and staff departments.

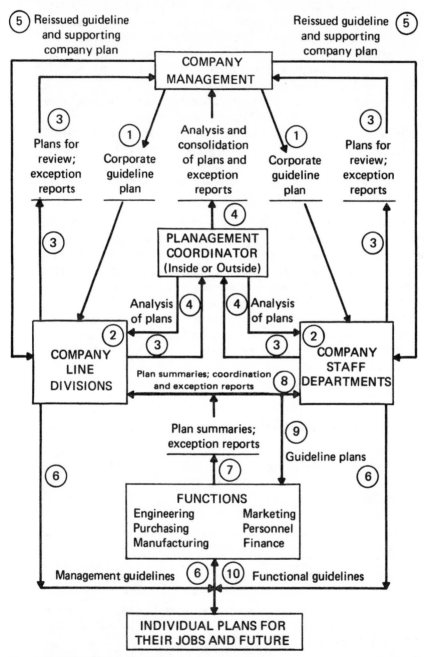

Figure 12. Salesman's plan–Section 4C: Key assumptions made for support from others (Form PA3).

	THIS	REPLACES
FILE:	0.4Cl	
DATE:	1/10/XX	
PAGE:	1 OF 1	OF

COORDINATION REPORT

Originator:
Distributor: R & D Department

Subject: Sales forecast and estimated market potential

OBJECTIVE:

To establish a more accurate estimate of the true market potential and market share by 2/1/xx.

ASSUMPTIONS (What, Who, When, Why)	SUPPORTING OBJECTIVE (What, Who, When)
That the company R & D department will have a more accurate estimate of my market's potential and that this estimate of potential will be provided to me by 1/31/xx. The reason for this is to get a better insight into my present market share, the value of penetrating the market, and possibly revising my forecast, as well as reappraising this office as a district office in view of the size of the market potential.	The R & D department agrees to support your assumption and has incorporated as an objective in our plan, to give you the data by 1/31/xx and will advise you by exception report if we cannot meet the date or cannot provide you the information you requested.

Confirmed by _____

Date _____ (Name and title)

Dept. _____

Figure 13. Flow chart of communications.

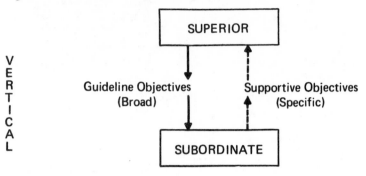

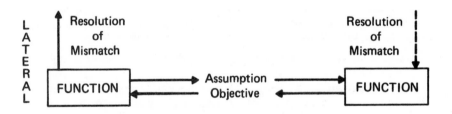

communication and coordination flow between the functional areas or other plans, regardless of the number of functions or plans.

Lateral communication and coordination should take place at the lowest possible level. An assumption should match the objective laterally in what is to be done, by whom, and why. Mismatches should be resolved at the lowest possible level of management.

Everyone who bases the accomplishment of his objectives and/or programs on assumptions that depend on someone else's making a needed input has the responsibility to insure that the needed input *is* an objective of the person or group he is depending on. The needed input should be written in a coordination report as an assumption, and a copy should be given to those responsible for supplying the input. The latter should confirm in writing their commitment to providing the needed input, attaching a copy of the stated objective. In case of a mismatch, it is up to the person making the assumption to resolve the difference. This procedure applies to both line and staff. (Use Planagement Form PA3, Figure 12.)

In order to use this communication and coordination approach, everyone who is responsible for accomplishing other-than-routine objectives should be equipped with a Planagement manual and be held accountable for contributing needed inputs. *This procedure applies only to major or creative types of assumptions and objectives, not to established routine ones.* Once the assumptions, objectives, communications, and coordination become established routine, this procedure would no longer be needed.

Granted, it takes a strong manager and management team to make the Planagement program work in an organization. A weak, complacent, or obsolete manager would not welcome this type of system. As a matter of fact, he would be unlikely to survive in an organization that makes the decision to identify and manage its potential through the growth and development of its people. Planagement was designed primarily for the growing person, professional manager, or member of a management team who wants to see the best in others and give the best he has.

13

The Professional Manager
and His Organization

BECAUSE OF the changing requirements for a manager, a new style of management and a different organizational structure are evolving. The new type of organization is led by a professional manager who operates with professional skill and the authority of earned prestige. He recognizes that the only real difference between companies is in the competence and dedication of their people, and so he considers himself to be primarily in the people business. He knows how to effectively blend the behavioral sciences with the techniques and tools of scientific management. The professional manager has developed a style of leadership that attracts and keeps the best key managers, who frequently have a strong entrepreneurial bent and therefore are very challenging to manage.

If present trends continue, anyone who wishes to become a senior manager in the next decade will have to become a professional manager capable of creating, guiding, and monitoring a highly dynamic, challenging, entrepreneurial organization. A profile of the professional manager is presented below. I suggest that if you wish to develop into a professional manager, you establish your own personal profile in order to compare it to the professional manager's profile. Then you will be able to identify your personal development gap and write a self-development program.

Profile of the Professional Manager

Management is evolving into an identifiable and respected profession. The leaders of this evolution, commonly referred to as professional managers, might be defined as those people who have acquired the ability to manage a situation or business without having had extensive experience with that situation or business. Some of the more important characteristics and skills of the professional manager are:

1. He realizes that the manager's primary responsibility and skill is in successfully understanding, guiding, building, and monitoring people and their relationships with one another.

2. The professional manager recognizes that the greatest unrealized potential exists in the human mind, and he develops a skill for working smarter, not just harder. He is able to teach this thinking/action skill to his management team so that together they can identify and manage individual and organizational potential for profit, growth, and satisfaction.

3. One of the key skills of the professional manager is his diagnostic ability—that is, his ability to ask the right questions of the right people at the right time. Through this technique he will be able to understand a situation and, equally important, obtain the answers and decisions needed to take action. In this way, people closest to the action and responsible for taking action will understand the situation better and have the satisfaction of participating in the decision-making process. As a result, they will be much more capable of, and committed to, making the decision happen.

4. The professional manager has an inquiring mind and is constantly searching for a new and better way of doing something. He understands the principles and uses the tools of scientific management, but always within a well-understood framework of the behavioral sciences. He utilizes a productive systems approach that integrates logic/fact/scientific tools/method with feeling/empathy/intuition/emotion/human understanding. He is a superior communicator and a good listener. He evaluates people by their direction and results, not by their position. The professional manager consistently sees the best in others and always gives the best he has.

5. The professional manager regards the successful development of his management team at all levels as his most important opportunity. He works toward creating an organization that constantly identifies potentials and challenging opportunities that provide

growth positions for his managers. He believes rewards should be commensurate with contributions.

6. He manages by example; has a clear, sound direction, strategy, and priority of values; and lives up to the standards of a professional. His philosophy of management is communicated in the missions, plans, policies, and practices he carries out, and his style is that of a leader who builds a company through building its people. His authority is based primarily on earned prestige rather than on the right to order, hire, or fire. His integrity is absolute—he may sometimes be wrong, but he is always honest.

7. The professional manager establishes a living organization and flexible structure so that he can anticipate and manage change. He regards change as an opportunity, not a problem. He is generally optimistic, with a belief in himself, others, his business, and the future.

8. The pro does many things well. He tends to be a generalist who understands how various disciplines such as marketing, selling, production, engineering, and finance interact to optimize profit and growth. To him, the whole is greater than the sum of its parts, and this synergy assists him to identify the expanding potential of his organization and manage it into being.

9. Perhaps one of the most important characteristics of the professional manager is his ability to make the complex simple. He possesses the vision to perceive the big picture, and at the same time has the needed discipline to see, analyze, and soundly manage the pieces that make up the picture. In other words, he not only knows what time it is, he is also able to organize to build the watch. Though the pro pays attention to detail, he does not become immersed in it. He is a skillful delegator who can get things done through other people regardless of reporting relationships. Organization is not a hang-up for him; it is rather a dynamic tool created to support the plan.

10. The professional manager has strong skills in planning, analyzing, organizing, and developing the minimum amount of information required to make the best possible decisions fast on a continuous basis, and successfully deploys controls to monitor progress and effect adjustments necessary to carrying out decisions made. The pro is superior at developing sound strategy because he realizes strategy has a crucial impact (70 percent plus) on the success of an enterprise. He views his enterprise with the kind of responsibility and courage the original entrepreneurs had.

The Professional Manager's Organization

Perhaps the most tangible product of the professional manager is the kind of organization he creates. This organization can take many forms, but it always evolves from the needs of the enterprise (as reflected in the documented plan), as well as the needs and capabilities of those who comprise the organization.

If there is a single key to managing profitability (optimum balance of profit and growth as measured by the continuing gain from the activity), it is the ability to place the right person in the right job at the right time. Should a gap exist between a man's skills and experience and the responsibilities of his job, the professional manager implements a tailored program of management development designed to reduce the gap as much as possible.

Another characteristic of the professional manager's organization is that it is dynamic. Since the organizational structure has been created out of the needs of the plan for the business and the people in the business, as these needs change, so will the structure. There is, however, a consistent striving toward the entrepreneurial concept of organization, which focuses on the individual as the plan-

Figure 14. Entrepreneurial organization structure.

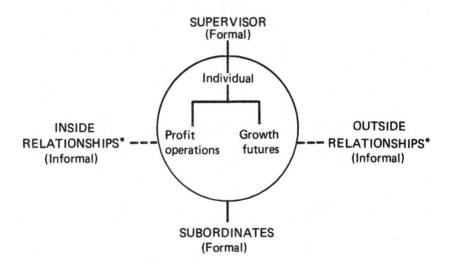

*Documented with a communication/coordination report.
Copyright © 1974, Planagement, Inc.

Figure 15. Entrepreneurial organization communications flow.

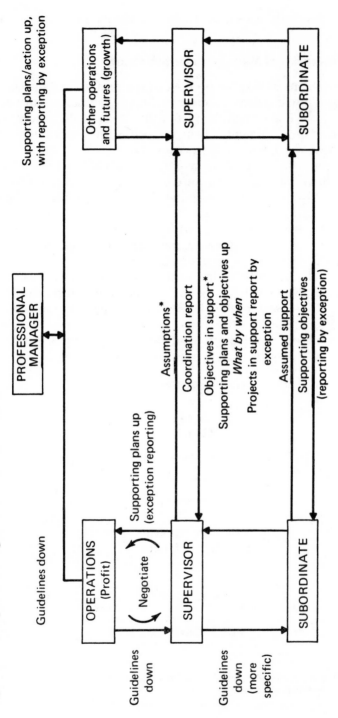

ning/management/profit/control center for his own area of responsibility. (See Figure 14.) The way this entrepreneurial organization structure might work is illustrated in Figure 15.

This type of dynamic, highly flexible, entrepreneurial organizational structure is needed for a variety of reasons. In our affluent society there are many highly educated people whose basic human requirements (physical, security, social, and recognition needs) have been satisfied to the point where they demand a job that allows them to "do their own thing." They want to be respected as individuals. They want the independence to accomplish their personal objectives and career plan along with meeting job and company objectives. Thus the organization that effectively combines personal objectives with job and organization objectives is in a much stronger position to attract such people than the organization that refuses to do this. Since these independent and competent people are self-reliant and are able to make better decisions faster and anticipate and react more rapidly to change, the organization that attracts and keeps them will also be able to make better decisions faster and manage change to advantage.

14

A Key to Profitability
Now and in the Future

A MANAGEMENT system that continually identifies, places, and maintains the right person in the right job is the key to profitability in an organization. It will produce continuing gain through the activities of growing people who want and are capable of handling more and more responsibility and challenge. To establish this management system, it is necessary to:

1. Define direction with regard to profit, profitability, and growth.

2. Establish a climate that is compatible with the chosen direction.

3. Create the concept and structure that will support the organization plan.

4. Structure good jobs that will attract and keep the people needed to accomplish the plan and its key objectives.

5. Identify the right people for the right jobs. This includes defining and managing any development gap that exists between an individual and his present job, or his future job as determined by his career plan and the needs of the company.

6. Institute a recognition and compensation program that objectively and fairly rewards performance and results.

7. Initiate an overall program of individual and management development that measurably taps the greatest unrealized potential,

creative abilities, and entrepreneurial spirit in employees. The program will continually redefine, enhance, and expand the original definition of direction, profit, profitability, and growth of both the individual and the organization (a closed-loop management system).

Direction, Profit, Profitability, and Growth

The first step in this management system is to establish sound direction. The guidance for identifying the proper direction for an individual or organization usually comes from a well-thought-out mission. (The importance of a mission and its relationship to profitability were reviewed in Chapter 4.) While the development of a sound mission is a challenging task in its own right, it is sometimes just as challenging to communicate the mission and resulting direction to those who must understand them in order to be able to act in meaningful support. This is where a written Planagement guideline plan can be of enormous help.

Communication, of course, is one of the most frustrating problems in management. There are many reasons why this is so, but the predominant one is the use of jargon which has so little meaning, or so many different meanings, that no common understanding is possible. When managers are asked to define such frequently used terms as *strategy, planning* and the *planning process, marketing versus sales,* and *profit, profitability,* and *growth,* they cannot agree on common definitions—sometimes they can't come up with any definitions at all. Do you have solid definitions of these vitally important management terms? Could you write your definitions down so that they could be understood by others? Many very skillful and competent managers either can't communicate their understandings or devise definitions that are full of errors.

For example, the most common definition of growth is: "increasing sales volume, profits, and return on investment." At first glance this might seem like a good definition; however, it is not, because you could accomplish all three of these increases by selling your assets until you disappeared up your own balance sheet. (Unfortunately, this has happened to many companies.)

The words *profit, profitability,* and *growth* differ importantly in meaning. *Profit* and *profitability* are often used interchangeably to denote output over input, or all revenues less all expenses equals profit or income; and *growth* is often confused with both. But all three terms have a precise and useful definition:

Profit is the income derived from revenues less expenses; it can be measured as a qualitative gain for a nonprofit, mission-oriented organization.

Profitability is a continuing gain from the activity, which is achieved by establishing an optimum balance of profit or other gain and growth of the enterprise. This concept applies to both profit and nonprofit organizations.

Growth is a combination of continuous increase in the assets employed in the enterprise and continuous increase in the return on those assets such that the enterprise will be able to attract all the assets required to accomplish its plan. (Assets are defined as people, money, materials, time, and space. The terms *assets* and *resources* are used interchangeably.)

The relationship of the three terms is illustrated in Figure 16. Growth, profitability, and profit are three phases of the business life/profitability cycle shown in Figure 17, and whichever one is emphasized determines management style.

Growth can take place anywhere in the profitability cycle, as illustrated by the new growth lines 1, 2, 3, 4, and 5 in Figure 17. The style of the manager who emphasizes this A phase is creative and entrepreneurial; he enjoys the challenge of building and making new concepts a productive and profitable reality. His primary focus is on identifying and managing potential, and he is effective—that is, he knows how to do the right things.

Profitability is the optimum balance between operations (profit) and futures (growth). To accomplish this, the skills and style of the professional manager are required (described in "Profile of the Professional Manager" in Chapter 13). The primary focus in phase B of the profitability cycle is on establishing a sound balance between managing the momentum of the enterprise and identifying and managing its potential. The B type of manager also balances effectiveness (strategy) with efficiency (operating).

Profit, which is maximizing results with what you have now, requires doing things better. The C type of manager is an administrator with a high degree of skill in doing things right (being efficient). His primary focus is on managing momentum in the best possible manner, using key operating ratios in order to achieve and control satisfactory results in a changing and possibly negative environment.

If these definitions are acceptable and helpful to you, you should make a decision on what your primary direction will be as an individual with an area of responsibility—or, if you are the chief executive officer of your company, what the direction of your company

Figure 16. The relationship of profit, profitability, and growth.

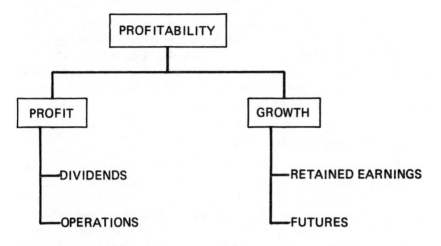

Figure 17. The business life/profitability cycle.

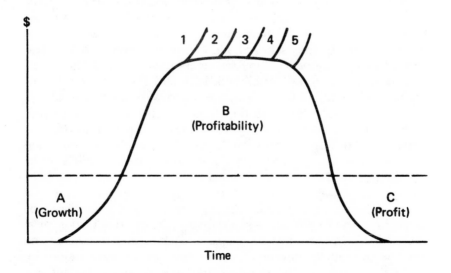

will be. In the latter case, your decision will determine the type of company you create and the results you achieve. And to a great extent, the direction of your company will determine the type of managers you attract and keep. Obviously, a builder will not be happy in a static situation where tomorrow is much the same as today and yesterday. The reverse is also true: someone who feels comfortable in a routine situation will be frustrated in a situation where the main ingredient is the challenge of the new.

Compatible Climate

Regardless of what decision you make, you will have to establish a strategy and a plan of action to make your decision an operating reality. Then you must create a climate that is compatible with, and supportive to, your plan. The importance of climate management was reviewed in Chapter 6. Suffice it to say here that the Planagement System works best in a climate where freedom is balanced with discipline, and that this type of climate can only be created where there is a belief in and respect for the individual.

Concept and Structure

You already know how essential it is to organize your resources in the best possible manner in order to accomplish your plan efficiently and realize its greatest possible potential. In the Planagement System, this organization is done in the ninth section of the plan—organization, delegation, and development. Here we are faced with a crucial management process, and unfortunately it is often hindered by the backward, ineffective, and even harmful ideas current in management. Many managers seem to think that structure is static, that once established, it should remain regardless of changes. They have a fixed idea about an ideal structure that always works in every situation, and they insist that people and plans conform to this so-called ideal. Quite frankly, I don't think this is a sound view of organization. In fact, I believe it's backward and usually results in a negative, static, restrictive climate that is a prime breeding ground for the obsolete manager.

In reality, there is no one perfect organizational structure that will work best for every plan, in every situation, and with every type of person. Any organization is a dynamic, living combination of at least three elements—people, plans, and changing situations—and must be continually adjusted. Other influences on organizations include the nature of the business, the style of the president, the chosen mission of the company, and the external environment. The organizational development process is a closed-loop system. First, management plans and establishes the direction and supporting plan of action. Then it identifies the tasks that must be accomplished to make the plan of action operational. The tasks are sorted into logical groups of related tasks, and form the accountabilities for different jobs. The groups are then arranged in a logical structure of organizational units of homogeneous tasks. At this point, the human talents required to manage the organizational units and individual tasks are summarized in position descriptions. The right people are matched with the right jobs.

Historical evolution also has an influence on sound organizational concepts and structure. A business will start with an original entrepreneur—that all too rare person who has both a dream and the guts to back it up with total commitment and a willingness to take risks. In this formative stage the organization will look like Figure 18, with the entrepreneur intimately guiding all three challenging divisions. The business is just beginning the A phase (growth) of maturity in the business life/profitability cycle. (See Figure 17.)

After a period of success and growth, the entrepreneur will start to feel the pressure of wearing too many hats. This is a crucial point in the evolution of a business, because to go from a one-man operation to a partnership or team operation is difficult, and many entrepreneurs are unable to make the business grow beyond themselves. But ideally, the entrepreneur will analyze the needs of his business and figure out what he is best at doing and what he is not so good at and/or doesn't like doing, and will hire staff accordingly. Perhaps his first step will be to acquire some marketing help and a staff administrative assistant. In that case, his organization will look like the classic organization of line and staff pictured in Figure 19.

As his business grows, the entrepreneur will perceive that additional functions need full-time managers, and he will probably organize along the traditional, functional lines shown in Figure 20.

Figure 18. The original organization.

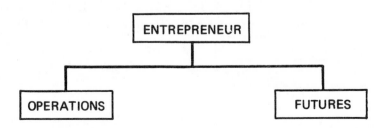

Figure 19. Line and staff organization.

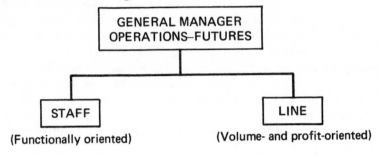

Figure 20. Functional organization.

Figure 21. Task organization.

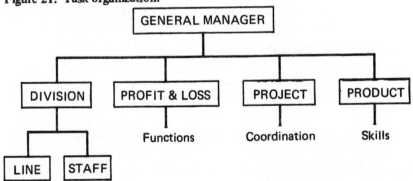

Because he is successful, the entrepreneur's business will start to attract competition, and in order to remain the leader in his chosen field, he will find it necessary to delegate more and more responsibility to others, including responsibility for profits. His organization may start to evolve from a functionally oriented organization to a task-oriented one. (See Figure 21.) There are many reasons for moving into this type of organization, including giving others the opportunity to create or run a business/profit center so they will develop into general managers and potential back-ups for the original entrepreneur. Now that the business is no longer dependent on one man for its survival and continuity, it is probably in the B phase of the business life/profitability cycle and requires the skills of a professional manager. Very rarely is the entrepreneur this man. In fact, at this point the entrepreneur will be a negative influence on the business he created if he does not relinquish it to the skills and talent it now requires. The balancing of operations and futures must now be

Figure 22. Possible future organization.

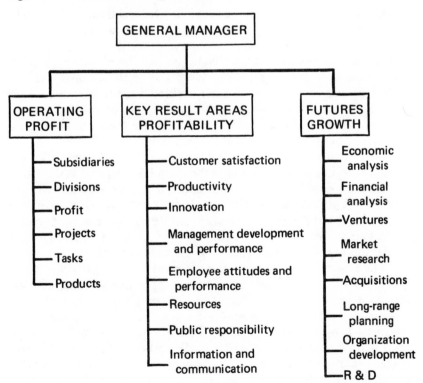

done over a very much broader base and should involve several key people (they might comprise "The President's Office"). In order to keep the optimum balance between profit, profitability, and growth, the organizational structure should probably look like Figure 22.

Now the organization is composed of a growing number of people and is becoming increasingly complex. To avoid the normal atrophy experienced by many large organizations, each job in the organization could be viewed as a business in itself, with each individual viewed as the planning/management center for his own area of responsibility. In other words, the individual would become the entrepreneur of his own job, and organizational structure would focus on the individual within the framework of the organization's direction as established by its guideline Planagement plan and practice. (See Figure 23.) Communications in this type of organization are depicted in Figure 24.

Job Structuring

Under the Planagement concept of organization, the normally fragmented and sometimes competing functions of planning, organization, personnel, and control are all integrated into a single function so the right person for the right job may be identified, placed, and maintained. (See Figure 25.) Once the organizational concept, approach, and structure have been decided on, the identified tasks to be done are combined with the kind of talent required to accomplish them, and these talents and tasks are converted into position descriptions with specific accountabilities.

In order to attract, place, and maintain the right person in the right job, and in order to provide for the job enlargement that stimulates both people and the organization, it is necessary to structure good jobs. One reason so many people are unhappy in their jobs is that their jobs are poorly structured. And unhappy people perform inadequately and change jobs frequently. So, how do you structure a good job that will attract and keep the best people?

The first requirement is to build a good company that has a fine opportunity for profit and growth and a positive internal climate. The next is for the management of the company to recognize the inescapable fact that people want to be defined and recognized as individuals. People today are telling institutions and organizations to "stop defining me the way you need me to be—define me as I am." Modern management must realize that work is not an instrumental act but a meaningful activity, and that workers have to be defined by their own needs as well as management's.

Figure 23. Planagement entrepreneurial organization.

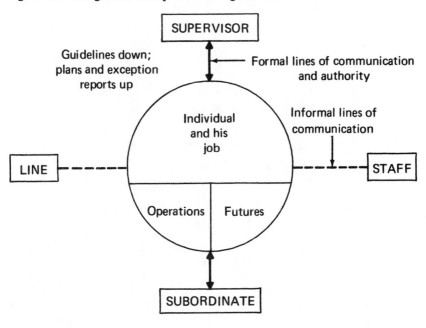

Figure 24. Flow of communications.

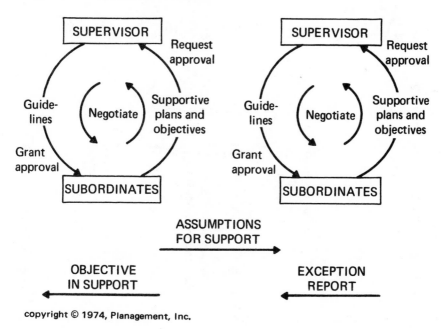

Figure 25. Planagement process: Placing the right person in the right job through the integration of the functions of planning, organizational development, personnel, and control.

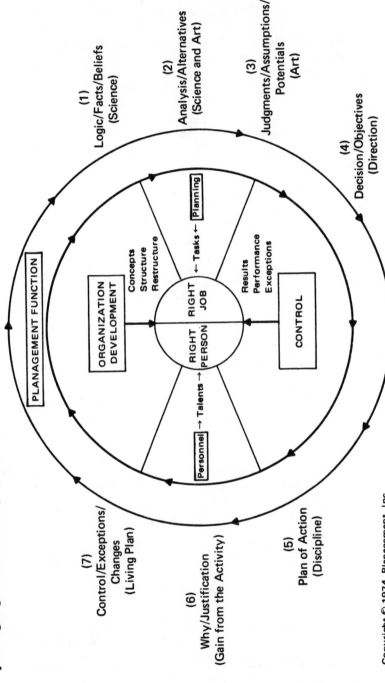

(1)
Logic/Facts/Beliefs
(Science)

(2)
Analysis/Alternatives
(Science and Art)

(3)
Judgments/Assumptions/
Potentials
(Art)

(4)
Decision/Objectives
(Direction)

(5)
Plan of Action
(Discipline)

(6)
Why/Justification
(Gain from the Activity)

(7)
Control/Exceptions/
Changes
(Living Plan)

PLANAGEMENT FUNCTION

ORGANIZATION
DEVELOPMENT

Concepts
Structure
Restructure

Planning

← Tasks ←

RIGHT   RIGHT
JOB

RIGHT   PERSON

→ Talents →

Personnel

Results
Performance
Exceptions

CONTROL

With this warning in mind, here are some ideas that can be used to structure a good job and some ways to implement the ideas using the Planagement System:

1. Establish direct feedback of results. Don't delay, because the longer the feedback takes, the less reliable it is. Feedback should not be merely a personal evaluation—and it should be given directly to the employee, not his boss.

A Suggested Action: Ask the employee to develop a written plan based on his job and then to report by exception to his supervisor. In this way, the employee would become the first auditor of his own performance and have the opportunity to make the needed corrections to manage change and accomplish the plan. Through the use of the exception report, the plan would be kept up to date and the employee would improve his skill for managing change to advantage.

2. Every job should have a client relationship. The employee should recognize that he has a customer to serve, that he doesn't exist to please his supervisor or to follow rules and procedures blindly. This customer can be an area, another department, or any element inside or outside the organization.

A Suggested Action: In the first section of his plan for the job, the employee would specifically define who his customer is and what key influences cause the customer to buy his products (reports, for example) and/or services (recommendations, for example). In some companies the staff department is required to sell its services to the line organization in competition with outside consulting and service groups. Needless to say, this has quite an impact on the attitude and performance of staff personnel.

3. Every job should have a learning function and an outside training program. A job should be structured so that at least 15 percent of it requires learning something new continually.

A Suggested Action: This learning function would be included in the job's accountabilities, and 15 percent of the employee's available time would be spent on it. The learning accountability would be converted into a specific objective in the plan and be supported by a written self-development and education program.

4. The person doing the job should have the right to schedule his own work as much as possible. He knows better than anyone else how to do his job.

A Suggested Action: As part of his written plan, the employee would prepare an operational schedule that would show, in order of priority, his objectives and supporting programs with key milestones.

This schedule would be reviewed and approved as part of the plan; once approved, it would be reported on by exception (as would the rest of the plan).

5. Every job should require a unique expertise so that the person doing the job feels he knows more about something than anyone else and could virtually serve as a consultant to others on his specialty.

A Suggested Action: As part of the plan (in the first section), the employee would list the capabilities, areas of distinctive competence, key resources, and skills needed to do his job well. Then he would relate these items to himself. Any gaps between the job's requirements and his capabilities would be bridged by his personal development program.

6. The person in the job should have control over his own resources. Give him a budget for his own operation and let him manage it. Once his budget (or expense account) is approved, he himself should control the expenditures.

A Suggested Action: One of the last parts of the plan written by the employee would be a section on the budget and resources he requires in order to accomplish his plan. The requested resources would be reviewed, possibly modified, and then approved as part of the plan. It would then be left up to the employee to manage and control the resources that have been allocated to implement his plan.

7. Direct communication is essential. People should be able to communicate with each other without having to hurdle organizational barriers. In most companies the organization chart sets the lines of communication, and the frequent result is overcommunication. There are many things in life that are better left unsaid, and sometimes the more you communicate, the less you get across. Passive, automatic communication is useless; only selected necessary information should be passed on.

A Suggested Action: A coordination/communication report would support this particular suggestion and make it a practical and operational reality. The employee would write down his assumed support from others—over whom he does not have control or authority— and then go directly to these people and persuade them to agree to his assumption and establish it as an objective in their own plans. The objective would be reported on by exception, as would any other part of the plan, except that in this case the reporting flow would be horizontal or diagonal rather than vertical. This powerful tool is based on the idea that management is getting things done through other people regardless of reporting relationships.

8. An organization that accepts the above seven suggestions can demand personal accountability—it can hold each employee responsible for his job and measure his performance objectively against predetermined standards. Frequently, companies measure not how well their employees are doing, but how well housebroken they are. You really can't hold anyone but an idiot responsible for an idiot job.

A Suggested Action: The job and its requirements would be written down so that everybody clearly understands what is expected. This position description would include general and specific accountabilities (responsibilities). These accountabilities, in turn, would have specific standards of acceptable performance that are clearly measurable. Without such standards, there is no objective way to appraise performance and the job would be about as satisfying as playing golf with no par. The suggested format for a sound position description includes (note how these relate to Section 1 of the Planagement System):

Definition of the job.
Purpose of the job, including primary results to be achieved.
Nature of the job.
Unique capabilities, resources, and skills required to do the job.
Products and services of the job.
Customers served and key influences that cause a decision to buy.
Organization, coordination, and communication responsibilities.
Cost/benefit analysis and summary.
Accountabilities—general and specific.

The structuring of a good and satisfying job within a good organization is becoming an increasingly important part of the manager's job. How well the manager meets this key responsibility will frequently determine his own success as well as his company's future.

The Right Person in the Right Job

In order to place and maintain the right person in the right job, you must identify the potential "right person" and that person's development needs. To accomplish this, it is very helpful to supplement the organizational structure and written job descriptions with a skills inventory of the people within the organization. This skills inventory should include each person's performance history, reported ambition, and Planagement career plan. (Ideally, every employee's career plan would be included in his personnel file.) An independent professional psychological evaluation could be considered as an additional tool. This type of evaluation can also help to identify employees' self-development gaps so that tailored training and development programs and compensation programs can be designed.

Without question, business managers are beginning to recognize the value of knowing and using the behavioral sciences to understand the whole person.* The employee doesn't begin to exist when he appears on the job in the morning and cease to exist when he disappears from the job at five o'clock. The job is only one of his activities, one of the pieces that make up his existence. Just as his job influences the other pieces, so do the other pieces have an impact on how he does his job. A manager who understands the whole person will be able to tell how well someone will perform a job. Human psychology is an important subject and well beyond the scope of this book; however, it would be a significant omission not to suggest that you become familiar with the behavioral sciences and use them in management.

The Practical Ideal Manager

Most managers recognize that the greatest opportunity for increasing profits and growth lies in increasing the effectiveness of their managers. The question is, how do we tap the potential that exists in our present managers?

Many people in the management development field think that a program should be tailored to the specific needs of a company and the style of that company's managers. Another school of thought believes there is a logical and universal management development program that will be productive in any company, at any time, and with any and all managers. Perhaps the most productive approach is to borrow the best from both theories.

On the basis of my experience in creating and assisting in the implementation of management development and compensation programs in a variety of companies, I believe there is a simple and practical approach that can be taken to develop managers in most companies. The first step is to identify the type of managers who will best support your company's plan. (Though this first step is logical,

---

* The concept of the whole person considers the mental, spiritual, social, and physical attributes of a person as being synergistically interrelated. This synergism can be either positive or negative, depending on the health and balance of the attributes and the value the person places on them.

it is frequently overlooked, with the predictable result that many management development programs lack specific direction and a basis for measuring their progress and contribution.) Unless you create a specific profile of the "practical ideal manager," there will be no identified target for people to work toward.

Once you have established the target, the next step is to carefully and thoroughly document each present and future manager's position description. Very often the manager does not have a good understanding of his job, and frequently the boss and the manager see the job differently—which makes an objective performance appraisal practically impossible.

Once all jobs are defined and understood, you can establish a profile of all managers (skills inventory), showing their strengths, weaknesses, skills, experience, and *ambition,* and compare these profiles with the job profiles. Any gaps will form the basis for formal, individually tailored management development programs.

This approach works just as well for preparing your managers for future positions as for increasing their performance in their present positions. The position descriptions you construct will not only provide a target for your existing managers but will also give you a standard for selecting the right person for the right job—whether it be from inside the company or outside. The descriptions will be of considerable help in your people planning, as well as providing targets for developing your managers for tomorrow's opportunities.

Recognition and Compensation Program

You cannot expect to have the right person in the right job at the right time unless you have an objective program of compensation. To establish a sound, integrated management development and compensation program is one of the manager's biggest challenges and opportunities. It is a truism that the growth and development of an organization directly depend on the growth and development of its people, and people expect to be rewarded for their efforts. An appropriate compensation package recognizes and rewards performance based on results and growth. (See Table 9.)

Individual and Management Development

An overall program of individual and management development that will measurably tap the unrealized potential, creative abilities, and entrepreneurial spirit in every person is needed to com-

Table 9. The interrelationship of position description, Planagement program, accountability management, individual development, salary administration, performance appraisal, entrepreneur compensation concept, and job enlargement.

Planagement Section:		One	Five	Eleven	Twelve and back to One
Function	Standard Position Description	Results-Oriented Position Description	Standard Objectives; Objective Section Plan Book; Performance Evaluation Form	Aids in Priority Setting; Justification/Results	Salary Administration; Update Position Descriptions
Manufacturing: Plant manager	To produce goods at high quality and low cost.	To maintain at least a _% quality level at a quality control cost that does not exceed _% of manufacturing costs less overhead.	To obtain a _% quality level at a cost of _% by December 31, 19__	1. Inventory cost savings $_ annually. 2. Income of _¢ per no. manufactured on specification times _ equals $_. 3. Quality control in budget $_ annually. 4. Less cost of $_ for equipment, $_ for time; net gain equals $_	_ additional points or $_ additional for accomplishments. Bonus relative to savings $_, bonus _% equals $_. Shared by involved managers.
Sales: Salesman	To increase sales and control costs.	To increase sales at least _% each year while reducing costs at least _% each year in relation to the sales gain.	To increase sales volume by at least _% and reduce sales cost a minimum of _% each year.	Overall profit to the company would be _% of volume of sales above standard job.	_ points job enlargement. Bonus would be _% of additional revenue over standard objective.

Finance	To maintain the designated management controls.	To review the established control reports at least annually and recommend at least two ways in which they can be simplified and time can be saved.	To review the forecasting reporting and install this report on an exception basis by November 30, 19__.	Hours spent in forecasting reports is about ___ annually at an overall cost of $___ per hour. This equals $___. Exception Report will cut this by _/_ saving approximately $___ annually.	Bonus to financial department is _% of $___ or $___. No salary points since this is a standard objective.
Personnel	To hire the needed people for the organization at the least cost possible.	To reduce the cost per hiring by at least _% each year (exempt).	To have Person/Position Form 117 completed at least two months prior to the need for a person (_% cost reduction)—this to be policy by April 1, 19__.	With the additional information, screening will be reduced from an average of _ to _ persons, saving $_ of the $_ now spent per person times _ hires per year equals $_.	_% bonus on savings $___. Salary points - due to _% over standard.
Materials and Distribution	To reduce purchasing costs to the maximum while maintaining the desired or required quality.	To not have purchasing department's cost exceed _% of total cost of items purchased.	To obtain at least a _% reduction of costs in the purchasing department by December 31, 19__. Maintain a maximum cost of _% each year thereafter.	1. Establish new standard that is _% better than average costs of industry's. 2. _% of sales value is purchase cost, which is $___ at _% saving is $___.	1. Job enlargements on salary equals _% more points for productivity. 2. Bonus at _% is $___.

Figure 26. Individual manager.

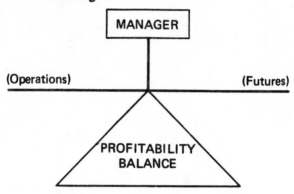

plete the Planagement profitability cycle. When this is accomplished, then the organization will be growing and changing as its people grow and change. This continuous process will redefine, enhance, and extend the original definition and plan of the business on the basis of its expanding potential for profit, profitability, and growth.

Figure 27. The organization's picture of the future based on its potential.

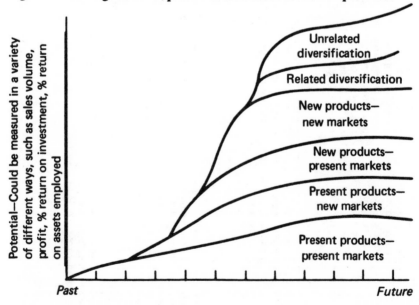

Figure 28. The conversion of an idea into a commercial reality.

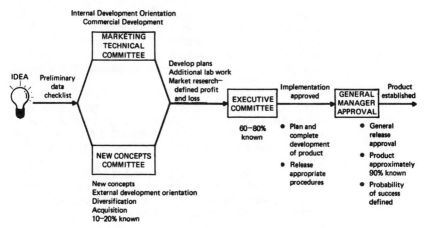

Copyright © 1974, Planagement, Inc.

If we were to snap a picture of the individual manager in this type of organization, we would see something like Figure 26. Collectively, the organization's picture might look like Figure 27.

The organizational unit that is responsible for the management of growth might be called the futures division or the company development division. This division would have as its primary function the conversion of an idea into a commercial reality. It would use the Planagement approach to develop a plan for the idea, which could become a new venture or, possibly, a new business in its own right. (See Figure 28.) A proposal for establishing a futures division could be submitted as a one-page summary plan, again using the Planagement System and format. (See Table 10 on the following page.)

In summary, then, a key to profitability now and in the future is to identify, place, and maintain the right people in the right jobs. In order to insure that both the individual and the organization maximize profitability, it is imperative to establish an internal, systematic, disciplined approach that identifies direction on the basis of inherent potential and solidly backs it up with dedication and development.

Table 10. Futures division proposal.

WHAT	1. The *Futures Division* would be a profit center, as would each functional area within this division.
	2. The *orientation* of this division would be *outside-inside* because of the increasing magnitude, impact, and speed of external changes. The need to quickly take ideas to profits has also increased.
	3. The *strength* of this division would be in the creative services it provides and the profits it generates. The *weakness* would be possible duplication of effort. *Action* would be to generate a profit within this division so that any duplication would be a duplication of profits and growth.
	4. The key *assumption* is that the needed personnel for this division are presently within the organization and will be made available as required. This will not increase costs since it is a reallocation of existing resources for increased effectiveness.
WHERE	5. The prime *objective* would be to prove the value of this division by generating a recognized profit by December 31, 19__. An additional objective would be that by 19__ at least 20 percent of the organization's volume and profits will come from products, services, and activities not now in existence.
HOW	6. *Strategy* basic to generating a profit would be to sell services and establish one profit center of at least $___ with an R.O.I.B.T. (Return on Investment before Tax) of at least *x* percent.
	7. *Alternate actions* would include doing this at a division level before doing it at the corporate level, doing it at a subsidiary level, not doing it, or doing it as a part-time responsibility of administrative services or another staff component.
WHEN	8. *Schedule:* Approval September 1, 19__; operational December 31, 19__; profitable December 31, 19__.
WHO	9. *Organization:* Four full-time people, plus two temporary people located in the general office.
COST	10. *Annual Budget:* $___ exclusive of overheads (budget is the investment).
PROFIT WHY RESULTS	11. *Results: x* percent of $___ direct before-tax profit, plus $___ indirect profits through services, plus a pool of entrepreneurial general managers who will provide future managerial talent. Also profit, growth, and diversification contributions.

Part V

Feedback and Measurement of Results

15

Review of a Manual Management Information System

ONE OF management's most important objectives is to establish a management information system that will provide the information needed to make good decisions. The need for such a system is becoming increasingly urgent in organizations because of the knowledge and information explosion we are experiencing. One of the manager's most potent tools for getting the information needed to make good decisions is the computer. Most computer programs have as their ultimate objective the creation and establishment of a total management information system (frequently referred to as M.I.S.). A great deal of money and incalculable man-hours have been spent on the pursuit of a total M.I.S., yet most management teams and computer experts agree that it is not yet a practical reality.

In consulting with a number of organizations and people engaged in M.I.S. programs, I discovered that the main reason no M.I.S. has been established is that there is no *manual* management information system. The computer can only pick systems that already exist, and apparently management teams have not yet figured out a manual system for decision making.

The Planagement Manual Management Information System

The truth of the matter is that most managers have not taken the time to figure out what information they need to make a decision. This situation was pretty well substantiated during the basic research phase of the Planagement System when a large number of managers were asked, "What is the minimum amount of information you require to make a sound decision, and in what order do you consider it?"

Not one manager had really given this question much thought, and consequently, none had a ready answer. Yet the answer to this question would contribute substantially to the structure and content of a management information system.

One of the primary objectives of the Planagement System was to establish a manual management information system that would provide managers with a tool for identifying, gathering, organizing, analyzing, and presenting the minimum amount of information required to make a sound decision and to assist in making the decision happen. The tool we were looking for would be applicable by any manager, at any level, to any situation, so managers would be able to consistently manage inconsistent situations to produce constant gain.

After analyzing the responses to the question asked about what information was required to make a decision, we created a model that provided, in logical sequence, the basic questions that should be considered in making virtually any decision.

Most managers make decisions based on numbers—the forecast less the budget equals the profit plan. Errors and changes, however, do not occur in numbers, but rather in facts, judgments, and actions. Unless a management information system deals with these factors in addition to numbers, it will be incomplete and, frequently, ineffective.

Most management information systems are predominantly numbers-oriented, which makes them far less productive than they might otherwise be. Thus, in most organizations a total management information system still does not exist, and a primary management need has not been met in a satisfactory manner.

For years, accountants have had common formats for identifying, gathering, organizing, analyzing, and presenting the numbers required for decision making. These formats include balance sheets, profit and loss statements, and a host of others.

What has been missing is a common format for managers to use to understand and communicate the logic and judgment they employ to establish the numbers and determine the actions required to make the numbers happen. The Planagement System provides this common format, together with a feedback system that anticipates and incorporates changes. It is based on the idea that decisions should be made primarily on this behind-the-numbers information rather than on the numbers alone.

The Planagement Manual Management Information System utilizes several existing numbers-oriented models, as well as key intangible factors. The system can be used both by individuals for their jobs and by teams for collectively managed areas of responsibility.

Each manager's plan would be composed of the summary of the plans developed by the people reporting directly to him and the summary of his own plan for his job. This consolidated summary would be submitted to his supervisor, and the process would be repeated until it encompassed everyone from top management to first-line supervisors. The process is shown in Figure 29, where:

- E's plan is a fusion of the plans of F, G, and H, and E's summary plan. His consolidated plan is summarized and submitted to A and, when approved, is reported on by exception.
- A's plan is a fusion of the plans of D and E and A's own plan. His consolidated plan is summarized and submitted to M; following approval, A reports on it by exception.

Figure 29. The Planagement manual management information system.

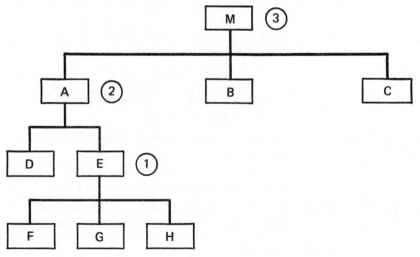

Figure 30. Plan summary for Crescent Company.

		THIS	REPLACES
	FILE:	00.	
PLANAGEMENT	DATE:	12/31/XX	
SECTION NUMBER	PAGE:	1 OF 1	OF

(What)   1.   Crescent is *defined* as a publicly held profit-making corporation with a *scope* of innovating, manufacturing, and marketing products and services to the distribution industry. The prime *mission* is to increase Crescent's growth by reducing distribution costs for customers using Crescent products and services.

2.   A strong profit squeeze exists in the *economy*, which will work both for and against the company. Labor rates are increasing, which is a plus because it encourages automation of distribution.

3.   The *strength* of the company is in its R & D capability and unlimited growth potential. Major *weaknesses* include a shortage of capital and increasing competition. *Action* is to raise capital through a stock sale, which will allow the company to develop a more complete product line at lower cost and thus increase its lead over competitors.

4.   Crescent's key *assumption* is that there will not be a recession. The most important *potential* is in the pooling concept.

(Where to go)   5.   The company's most important *objective* is to meet or exceed its five-year forecast with primary emphasis on increasing the assets employed with at least an x percent ROABT.

(How)   6.   Crescent's *strategy* is to increase sales by identifying and maintaining a captive pool, and by marketing a total system and service capability as opposed to component sales.

7.   The most important *program* is to increase market penetration.

(When)   8.   The schedule is for Crescent to obtain at least an x percent market share by December 31, 19xx.

(Who)   9.   The most significant change in the *organization* will establish a Corporate Development (Futures) Division. This new profit center will be managed by a vice-president.

Figure 30 (cont.)

(Cost) (How much)	10.	The current operating *budget* will be increased by $x,xxx,xxx in order to accomplish this plan.
(Benefit) (Why)	11.	The most important results from the plan will be to increase sales by $xx.x MM, increase net profit before taxes by $x.xxx MM, and establish a return on assets that averages at least *x* percent over the next five years and is increased by at least *x* percent each year.

- M's plan is a consolidation of the summary plans of A, B, and C, and M's plan. M's plan would be summarized in such a manner as to identify, gather, organize, analyze, and present the minimum amount of information to make the needed decisions and effectively control the area of responsibility he has been assigned.

The Manual Management Information Format

Now that you have established a format for organizing and communicating needed information, you should ask yourself how you will identify the minimum amount of information to be communicated in the summary of your plan. There is no one answer to this question, since everyone has a different level of information requirement for decision making. Some people feel comfortable only if they have all the information readily available, including all the supporting data. Others want a simple, brief summary such as the one in Figure 30. Some won't make a decision until all the facts are known; others tend to decide on the basis of their gut feelings about a situation.

Even though there is no definitive answer regarding the minimum information required to make a decision, a supervisor and subordinate must agree on a plan for planning or the planning will probably never be completed. They should at least concur on the plan's format, the questions the plan should answer (the content to be included), and the approximate length of the plan and its summary. If they decide to use the Planagement plan for planning, they have an already established format and basic content (the questions contained in each of the Planagement sections).

It is suggested that the summary of the Planagement plan be between 20 and 30 pages and that pictures, charts, graphs, tables, and flow diagrams be used for a concrete presentation. The Planagement Summary Outline should be the starting point, tailored with supplemental questions and answers. Any Planagement questions that are not applicable, of course, should be dropped.

The reason I have suggested a liberal inclusion of charts and diagrams is that pictures are one of the best techniques for communicating a plan. When we see pictures in our mind and transfer these visions to other people through words, much is lost in the translation. Therefore it is valuable to communicate your mind's-eye view in the form of a picture. (See Figure 31 for a picture of the Cresent Company business.)

The successful transfer of knowledge to others is perhaps as difficult as the gathering and processing of that knowledge (in some cases, more difficult). One important guideline to follow in overcoming the celebrated communications gap is to write your plan summary so clearly and concisely that someone unfamiliar with you or your business would have a good understanding of both if he read it.

Your summary should include only those factors that will have major influence on the results the plan is to achieve. As we saw in Chapter 9, it is usually 20 percent of the items that control 80 percent of the results, and it is these 20 items out of 100 that should be included in your summary. The other 80, which you might have to consider in order to gain the needed insight into the basic 20, could be included in your supporting plan.

The supporting plan is normally kept in Sections 1 through 11 of a person's Planagement manual, which is organized in the same way as the Planagement *Model*. The summary of the plan is filed in Section 0 at the front of the manual. (Refer back to Figure 30 for an example of a summary plan.) The primary purpose of making the summary is to select out of the supporting plan the minimum amount of information required to communicate the plan, make a decision in regard to the plan, and then manage and control the plan. It is the summary of the plan that will be reported on by exception. This keeps to a minimum the amount of information that is communicated for decision making and control.

There are several valid ways to develop a sound summary of your plan. One is to consider only the five or six most important elements under each of the basic questions and to limit the narrative sections to a maximum of three paragraphs. The key result areas concept (described in Chapter 9) is a valuable technique you can use

Figure 31. Flow diagram of the Crescent Company business.

Originator: J.A.
Distribution: Crescent Planning Book Holders (Code A)

	THIS	REPLACES
FILE:	0.1A	
DATE:	7/31/XX	
PAGE:	2 OF 2	OF

4. Flow Diagram of the Business

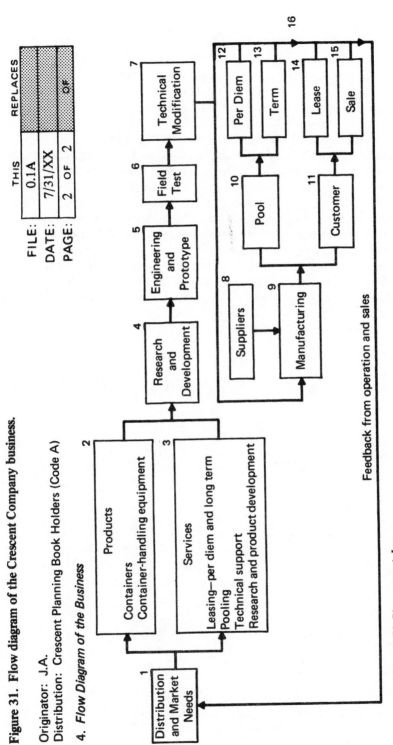

to get a grip on those basic "dials" that control the results. Key operating ratios are of crucial importance in controlling a plan in changing times, because if these basic ratios are maintained, then the forecasted results will be achieved.

Whoever uses the Planagement System for planning, managing, and controlling himself, his situation, and his future has established his own manual management information system for making better decisions faster and assisting in making those decisions a productive reality. When all the managers in an organization utilize the Planagement System individually and collectively, the organization will have a manual management information system that can be effectively supported by the computer. Eventually, the organization may decide to establish a total management information system that is a combination of the Planagement Manual System and the supporting computer model. Both will be dependent on the manual plan, the accurate perception of changes and exceptions, and the quality of individual judgment and discipline.

16

The Pursuit of Excellence

That man is a success who has lived well, laughed often and loved much; who has gained the respect of intelligent men and the love of children; who has filled his niche and accomplished his task; who leaves the world better than he found it, whether by an improved poppy, a perfect poem or a rescued soul; who never lacked appreciation of earth's beauty or failed to express it; who looked for the best in others and gave the best he had.
—ROBERT LOUIS STEVENSON

How DO YOU perceive yourself? Everyone has the capability to pursue excellence, but few people make the commitment, take the actions, and pay the price required to live up to their potential. One of the most important premises of this book is that people will improve themselves if they are shown how to do it in a way that makes sense to them. It is elitist and untrue to suppose that only a chosen few are capable of mastering themselves and leading others. It is also foolish, because present requirements and challenges virtually compel us to expand considerably the number of leaders and entrepreneurs who can manage and control themselves, their situations, and their futures.

Self-Image

How you perceive yourself will determine whether or not you realize your greatest potential. Imagine a spectrum of behaviors, with the *comfort zone* at one end and the *challenge zone* at the other. The comfort zone represents complacency and momentum; the challenge zone represents excellence and the fulfillment of potential. When confronted with a choice between comfort and challenge, people often make an automatic, subconscious decision. The self-image a person has will contribute in large measure to the progress he can and will make toward the achievement of excellence.

If you have a good self-image, you probably already know that in the pursuit of excellence it is the pursuit itself that counts; the effort to excel becomes its own reward. You also probably know that anyone who chooses to strive for excellence will often find himself the sole spectator of his effort. The only satisfaction he can count on absolutely is that of knowing he *has* done his best, *is* doing his best, and will always do his best.

If you are not exactly sure what your self-image is, or if you think it lies somewhere between these two extremes, remember that it is possible to experience resurgence any time you choose to. One of the most serious obstacles to progress is the tendency for people to wait for someone else to take action. Scapegoating is a favorite device of those who would rather blame the establishment for their problems than recognize that they themselves are responsible for improving their lives.

Incidentally, there is another factor which can be as important as self-image: the position an individual has with regard to the hierarchy of human needs. If a person has not satisfied his physical needs and his needs for security, social acceptance, and recognition, then it is unlikely he will be ready to self-actualize and pursue his own potential with resulting excellence.

The Four D's

Assuming you agree that individual resurgence is an individual consideration, I would like to suggest a formula you can use to accomplish internal and external changes. I call it the "four-D" formula.

The first of the four D's is *drive*. Drive frequently determines the distance a person will travel during his lifetime—in fact, some people feel that drive is everything. All of us have heard the common expression, "He really has drive—he's bound to be successful."

But success often depends as much on the second D as it does on drive, because all the drive in the world will be of little avail if it is not harnessed to a sound, well-defined *direction*. Direction channels drive into meaningful accomplishments. It is truly sad to see a hard-driving person, or a great and energetic organization, going off in all directions so that progress is painfully slow or negligible. You cannot make consistent progress without a "grand design." In fact, the expenditure of energy with no clear goal in mind is often counterproductive, if not destructive.

The third D is *discipline*, which frequently is the catalyst that unites drive with direction. Without self-discipline, people are stranded between their goals and their own inertia.

The fourth D is *development*—the continuous self-development that produces constant growth. The growth and development of an organization or a nation are directly dependent on the continuous growth and development of its people.

Reaching the Top

"How do I reach the top?"

"Now that I've reached the top, what do I do next?"

These two questions are frequently asked by those who are ambitious and those who are experiencing boredom and letdown in their success.

First of all, there is no such thing as *the* top. One person's life's goal is another person's misery. With that word of caution, it can be said that the top in business generally means the most senior manager's position, which in the case of a specialist would be the vice-president of a function, and in the case of a professional general business manager, the presidency with chief executive officer responsibility.

How do you reach the top? First, identify what job you would most like to have in the future. Then work toward the next job that is a milestone toward your ultimate objective. Your target should be reasonable and attainable. Equally important, it should suit you personally. Its responsibilities should provide you with challenge and satisfaction. Unless you have both of these, the job—regardless of title or prestige will probably not be a worthwhile, productive, or happy experience for you.

Many people rise to the level of their own frustration—observed frequently as their level of incompetence (the Peter Principle)—and instead of reaching a dream, they find themselves a nightmare. So don't rashly decide on the top you will strive toward. First, learn to know yourself pretty well, including what you really would enjoy doing and can do well. You might find it helpful to write a description of the type of situation you want to work in and then examine existing jobs in your company or chosen field to see how they compare to your ideal.

Once you have discovered your "compatible" next position, you should identify the gap between your present capabilities (you might write these down as well) and the job's requirements; this gap becomes your personal development plan. Repeat this process of examining who you are, where you want to go, and what you need to do to achieve your goal until you do reach the top.

Once you're there, you may very well find yourself wondering, "Now that I've reached the top of my profession—or my company— what do I do next?" There is always a certain poignancy to reaching the summit because the intense, energizing struggle is over and the person who "has it made" frequently feels unchallenged and bored. He really isn't enjoying his success, but he is fearful of losing what he has worked so hard to achieve.

One answer is to consider bringing along a replacement. Admittedly, this suggestion is not usually accepted with great enthusiasm, but it really does make sense for three reasons. First, the best way to learn a subject better is to teach it to someone else. Second, it is greatly satisfying to structure your knowledge and experience so that others can utilize it. This is a way to multiply yourself, to achieve an immortality of sorts—which is certainly better than being a one-man show that is in danger of dying when you do. One of the most important responsibilities of a manager is to be a good teacher. The manager who advances has usually mastered this important skill. He realizes that teaching is not knowing all the answers, but knowing the right questions to ask at the right time. This ability is something he can teach to the people who work for him.

The third reason is the fundamental principle that the growth and development of the enterprise are directly dependent on the growth and development of its people. If you teach the one below you, and he teaches someone else, and so on, you will then have a dynamic organization that attracts (and keeps) constantly growing and increasingly productive people. Such an organization has to be profitable and expanding.

The Educated Person

In a very real sense, the pursuit of excellence requires us to view life as a constant educational experience. We might, therefore, identify one engaged in the pursuit of excellence as a truly educated person. But—what is an educated person?

One of the most emotionally charged controversies is over what constitutes a true education. Some people are of the opinion that to be educated you must have attended school and received a degree that says you are now educated. Others feel a degree is not proof of education but only a piece of paper that certifies you have a smattering of fragmented facts and opinions. These people believe "the school of hard knocks" is the only practical academy.

Frankly, I don't think this is much of an argument. Both an academic education and experience have value, and are stronger when combined than alone. Let's face it, we have all met clods who have as their only claim to fame a degree—sometimes an advanced degree from a prestigious university. That piece of paper did not alleviate an obvious stupidity combined with an inability to perform. By the same token, we have all met pompous know-it-all graduates of the school of hard knocks who constantly refer to their twenty years of experience in the business. When we explore their knowledge of the business, we find they really have had one year of experience twenty times over. Then there are those rare people whom we immediately recognize as being several cuts above the ordinary. Somehow they have acquired a superior education.

Perhaps if we take a good look at some of the recognized characteristics of the educated person, we can learn more about the process that contributed to his personal development.

1. He has confidence—not that he knows he has all the answers but that he has the capability and self-discipline to get the needed knowledge to make a sound decision and to take the proper actions.

2. The educated person is well aware of J. Carl Humphrey's definition of greatness and lives by it: "The potential for greatness lies within each of us—it is simply our best." The educated person has developed the ability to see the best in others and give the best he has. He is a professional in every respect.

3. An open, inquiring, growing mind is a readily identifiable characteristic of the educated person. He does not hold prejudices, but views situations and people with an objective mind that seeks only the truth, the best, and the fair. He is a giver and a builder, never an exploiter.

4. Another characteristic is his ability to listen to all information and then apply analytical discipline to develop an independent, objective conclusion. In addition, he will be a skilled communicator.

5. An educated person will never laugh at new ideas or say that something is impossible, it cannot be done. His outlook is positive; he has faith that improvements can, should, and will be made.

6. You will not be able to sell an educated person on magic, luck, or happenstance because he knows that progress depends on consistency of purpose, direction, and the discipline to take action to make the right things happen.

7. Perhaps one of the most important aspects of an educated person's makeup is his ability to analyze himself objectively, identify his most important strengths, and then build on these strong points.

8. The educated person knows the value of good habits and understands how to form them.

9. Another vitally important skill of the educated person is his acquired ability to understand important differences. An example of this ability is reflected in the prayer, "Oh, Lord, help me to recognize those things I can change and those things I cannot change, and grant me the wisdom to know the difference."

10. While the educated person tends to be imaginative, he also is inclined to cross-examine his daydreams, selecting out the good ones to make them a practical, productive reality.

11. A truly educated person understands the learning process and continually applies it in his daily life. He knows that education is a journey, not a destination. He is teacher-oriented and willing to share his knowledge.

12. An ability to see and love the beautiful is another trait of the educated person. No matter how bleak a situation may be, he is able to identify the best and the beautiful in it.

Time Management

Besides a true education, anyone who is pursuing excellence will also need certain basic skills that can be used to advantage in virtually any situation. Take, for example, the skill of managing time. This is fundamental because it is the management of time that frequently determines success or failure. If time-wasting is your weakness, then you should read one of the many fine books on time management or attend one of the highly regarded workshops that help people manage their time better.

A good practice you can use right now to better manage your time is to list the six most important actions you should accomplish tomorrow in their order of importance. Tomorrow, complete them one at a time, starting with the most important. Though this daily time management approach seems simple, it is estimated to increase efficiency by up to 50 percent or even more.

Communication

A second vitally important skill that should be developed in order to pursue excellence is the ability to communicate well, both orally and on paper. Few gaps between people are more frustrating than that of the communications gap. This particular gap has several important dimensions. First of all, because of built-in biases it is difficult for us even to communicate objectively with *ourselves*. The problem is multiplied when we attempt to explain ourselves to others. Second, because of our biases we often find it easier to talk than to listen. As a result, we usually remember less than 10 percent of what we hear, and we frequently substitute our own interpretation for what was really said. We also seem to have a tendency to make the simple complex.

Finally, communications are sometimes garbled by physical expressions and movements. We often rely for our interpretations more on the tone of someone's voice than on the words he is saying. Our own moods may block our ability to understand what is being said, or we may just turn the other person off.

Bridging the communications gap is hard because it demands both self-discipline and empathy—not easy qualities to develop. Here are ten guidelines for improving your skill in communicating:

1. Periodically obtain an outside, objective appraisal of yourself, either by conducting an opinion survey among those who work for you and with you, or by utilizing a professional outsider who can give you feedback and insight.

2. Document in writing your personal philosophy (Section 1 of your Planagement plan) and constantly monitor the compatibility of your actions with your philosophy. Any deviations will provide valuable guidance for managing by example and convincing others that you mean what you say.

3. Make integrity one of your strong principles, because if people don't believe what you say, they won't hear what you say. They will second-guess you, and you will not be able to communicate.

4. Accept it as a basic law that the responsibility for communications rests with the *communicator*. In other words, if you do not communicate with someone, it is your fault, not his.

5. Train yourself to listen well. There are many good books and proven techniques for improving your listening skill. In fact, this is such an important skill that several colleges have established courses in listening for full credit. We were given two ears and one mouth for good reason.

6. Cultivate an open and inquiring mind. Learn to ask more questions and give fewer answers. If you acknowledge in your own mind that the other person may have a better idea than you, you will

hear him out. If you exchange one dollar with someone, you will have gained nothing; but if you exchange one idea with someone, you will be at least one idea richer, and perhaps this one new idea will produce several more valuable ones.

7. If you are not sure what the other person means, ask him to explain it again, and, if necessary, again. He probably won't resent your inquiry; he is more likely to appreciate it as an expression of your interest in what he is trying to say.

8. When dealing with a new or hard-to-understand thought, write it out. There is good reason for believing our brains are closer to our fingers than to our mouths, because we almost always better understand and remember what we write than what we hear (or say). The more senses we use to absorb or convey a piece of information, the more likely we are to remember (or communicate) it.

9. Develop a habit of genuine interest in the other person. This is not easy, because basically we are most interested in ourselves and, let's face it, some people are just plain bores or incompatible. Nevertheless, if you try to be interested in what the other person is saying, you will often be pleasantly surprised by what you learn. An additional dividend is that when you treat others with interest, they will become more interested in you.

10. Make a strong, consistent effort to improve your use of language. There is a correlation between success and command of the English language. People who express themselves well, both orally and in writing, are more likely to reach the top.

As you increase your communication skills, you will notice a corresponding increase in your ability to absorb knowledge. You will be able to more rapidly acquire, process, and apply information and ideas. The Planagement System will help you use your mind's decision-making capability, but this skill will be very much dependent on your ability to communicate effectively (learn the right facts and ideas) and efficiently (express the facts and ideas right).

Capitalizing on the Positive

The skill to identify and capitalize on strengths and opportunities is invaluable. While the ability to solve problems is important, it is even more important to be able to discern positive factors and to use them to reduce or overcome problems and weaknesses. It is easier to do this if you have an optimistic point of view. Strange as it may seem, if you anticipate and expect the best, the chances are that you will achieve more. By the same token, if you anticipate and expect the worst, you increase the chances for disaster.

Creativity

One of our greatest resources as human beings is our capacity to create. Many people feel that creativity is a rare gift few people have been blessed with at birth, but actually everyone has creative potential. You can increase your personal creativity by understanding what creativity is and using the right concepts and tools to develop it.

Creativity is a uniquely human attribute and, properly channeled, can bring both the supreme satisfaction of accomplishment and rich monetary reward. The people and organizations that stand out in their chosen field are the ones that come up with the new, the different, the better—the idea, product, or service that becomes the standard. Here is one definition which may help you to more clearly understand this "shadow of the substance": Creativity is a positive mental attitude with the synergistic skill of uniquely combining known elements while at the same time challenging the unfamiliar.

As this definition indicates, the capability for creativity is within our minds and can be developed by using our mental processes in a certain disciplined manner. Though creativity is more an art than a science, it is an art that can be learned—and taught.

Researchers have identified certain characteristics that are almost always present in the creative person.

1. He has a thirst for knowledge and an ability to process that knowledge so that it yields new and useful insights.

2. The truly creative person does not merely generate ideas; he is just as capable of taking action on them. The action taken frequently modifies and strengthens the idea, or generates new ideas. Thus the creative process is a continual process.

3. He is not limited to seeing things as they are; he sees what could be. Once when Michelangelo was walking through a stone quarry, he stopped before a large block of marble and said that he saw an angel imprisoned in it. He later chipped away at the block of marble and "released" the angel, which became one of his many masterpieces.

4. The creative person has drive, direction, and self-discipline. These characteristics are supported by courage and a tenacity of purpose that sees an idea through to completion.

5. An uncompromising intellectual honesty is another key strength of the creative person.

6. He is entrepreneurial-oriented; he will take a needed risk.

7. He is optimistic, with a strong positive attitude.

8. He is superior in his judgment and in applying common sense.

9. He is enthusiastic, possessing a zest and love for life.

10. The creative person is enterprising; he will challenge the unknown.

11. He is also persuasive—skilled in selling people on his ideas and inspiring action with sound reasoning.

12. The creative person is outgoing; he normally has good people skills and an ability to encourage people and ideas to grow in his presence.

13. He is dynamic, healthy, vital, and energetic, with a sound balance between exercising the mind and exercising the body.

14. He has superior conversation and writing skills, together with a superior knowledge and use of language.

15. The creative person possesses an open, inquiring, expanding mind. He balances this freedom of mind with the self-discipline necessary to take action.

16. He has the ability to anticipate change and the versatility to take advantage of what he did not plan on.

17. He is engaged in a constant pursuit of excellence. Though the creative person will strive toward the perfect—the ideal—his efforts will be realistic, practical, and measurably productive. He will be impatient with his progress, but patient in his pursuit.

18. Individuality and imagination are additional traits of the creative person, along with a good sense of humor, which is often needed to alleviate disappointment and prevent discouragement.

Few creative people have all these characteristics, of course, but if you work on those you lack, you will inevitably become more creative. The effort will be well worth it, because there are few greater satisfactions than coming up with a truly creative idea and then making that idea a productive reality. The ability to create and implement sound, new, productive ideas is the basis for establishing a successful business and living a full life.

Since the source of creativity is your own mind, one of the many benefits to be gained by exercising your mind is increased creativity. One technique that will stimulate the creative powers of your mind is called brainstorming. The purpose of brainstorming is to generate as many ideas as possible, and the steps used might be summarized as follows:

1. Clearly, correctly, and completely define a problem in writing.

2. List all the known facts about the problem.

3. List and use all important sources of information that relate to the problem in order to gather additional facts, judgments, experiences, and ideas.

4. Write down all the information gathered from the sources listed in Step 3.

5. Generate as many ideas as you can—individually and/or in a group. Do this without the brakes of judgment—that is, do not try to decide at this point whether an idea is good or bad. There are four basic rules in brainstorming: no negative thinking; the wilder the idea, the better; a large number of ideas is essential; combination and improvement of ideas is the primary goal.

6. After generating all of the ideas you can, rank them according to their feasibility, value, effectiveness, and suitability.

7. Develop an action plan for the best ideas, including estimated time, cost, materials, and other resources required. Decide who would have to do what, when it needs to be done, and the sequence of actions (with dates) required to make the idea a reality, together with the gain to be achieved.

8. After completion of the above seven steps, you will very often have a creative solution to the problem (or even a redefinition of the problem) that you did not initially think of. Probably one of the reasons brainstorming has proved to be such a valuable technique is the synergism that results from combining ideas. Usually one good idea sparks another, and the two in combination are of more value than either alone.

Another technique to stimulate creativity is to change your pattern of thinking. If you think in new ways about what has existed in the past or is present now, you may find yourself seeing things as they might be rather than as they are. The steps used to think in new ways are:

Associate—relate one element to another.

Combine various elements in new or different ways.

Adapt—an example is the extension of records and cassettes originally developed for entertainment to instruction.

Substitute—what different material or source of energy could you use in your business?

Magnify—think how to make things larger and consider the benefits of size.

Minimize—the miniature transistor is an example.

Rearrange—turn things around (fur linings in cloth coats, for example).

All the above steps will exercise your mind and increase your creative capability. They may even generate that "unbelievably great idea."

A third technique involves the use of tension and intentional opposites to stimulate creativity. A creative synergism often results from combining opposites. If you find yourself "on the horns of a dilemma," you may feel you have to choose between the two alternatives; but in fact, the most creative solution may be to borrow elements from each of them. If there is a key to constructive creativity, it is balance: the ability to know what time it is and also know how to build the watch.

One of the best examples of balanced creativity is the United States, which was founded on the challenging combination of individual rights and majority rule. The Planagement System—which is based on a balance between freedom and discipline—was also developed on this principle.

Note, however, that this creativity technique can be harmful when carried to extremes. A person who constantly strains himself by trying to see both sides of every question or utilize every extreme element may find that his creative capacity—like the candle burned at both ends—"will not last the night through."

In summary, if you wish to be a leader, you cannot leave your creative capacity to chance. Being creative is hard work and requires a great deal of self-discipline. It is a never-ending process, because if you become complacent, you will stop growing and perhaps become obsolete.

Persuading Others

Dealing with people, teaching, selling, and persuasion are all important skills to master since they are the lubricants that will move you toward the accomplishment of your plan. Each one of these skills is a subject in itself and requires a great deal of study and practice to master. As food for thought, consider the following guidelines:

1. Know in advance what you are going to say. Give some thought to the questions and objections that are likely to be raised, and have your answers ready.

2. Be constructive. Stress the merits of your own viewpoint, not the flaws in someone else's. Acknowledge the valid points of another's proposal before you refute it.

3. Know your audience. Understand the tastes, temperament, background, and plans of the people you would persuade.

4. Harness their desires. State your case in terms that show the listener how he can achieve what *he* wants by doing what *you* want.

5. Be specific. Don't try to sell an idea without first carefully estimating what it will cost, what it will save, and what it will achieve. This type of cost/benefit analysis is essential for identifying the gain from the activity, justifying its existence, and attracting needed support.

6. Be convinced yourself. If you don't believe in or use what you're selling or teaching, no one will believe you.

7. Avoid scare tactics. Attempts to pressure people into a decision by impressing upon them how dreadful a mistake they will be making if they reject it can backfire. Give your listener the opportunity to raise objections.

8. When objections come, welcome them. You can't overcome resistance until you know where and why it exists.

9. Beware of saying too much. Many a salesman has made a sale, and then gone on to talk his customer out of it. Once someone has been sold on your plan or point of view, get up and get out—or go on to the next point, which should be of equal or greater value than its predecessor.

The Paradox of Power

Once you are successful in your pursuit of excellence, it is incumbent on you to master the skill of constructively managing your accrued power. To manage power soundly, you must first understand the paradox of power, as represented by the following story.

"I want to be president of this company more than anything else in life! " This statement was made several years ago by an executive vice-president. Everyone present could see from his tense face that he really meant it. He looked absolutely stunned when asked why he wanted the job.

After a moment, he answered by saying, "I want the job because of the power that will be mine from being president of the company. I will be able to run it my way and get rid of the people who have been getting in the way of the progress we should be making."

This response is not exaggerated; frankly, it is not at all uncommon among hard-driving, dedicated executives who focus their efforts on getting the top job in their companies. What is interesting is what happened to this executive and his company after he was successful in reaching the president's office through an extremely vicious struggle. He failed, and hurt himself and his company very badly.

In exercising his power and prerogatives as president, he created a very negative climate in the company. His insistence on one-man dominance, backed up by his frequently invoked authority to hire and fire, betrayed his lack of respect for people. Because he felt that the majority couldn't think for themselves, he was constantly telling others what to do and then tightly controlling them. He generated such a lack of trust and confidence that communications were poor to nonexistent. "Do as I say, not as I do," was his dictum, and he surrounded himself with weak yes-men who preferred to agree with him rather than make a decision or take an action. The management philosophy and politics in his company was "do it to others before they do it to you."

It doesn't take much imagination to get the picture of what was happening in the company managed by this power-positioned and power-oriented president. The question is, why did this man fail? It wasn't because he was stupid actually, he was highly intelligent, well educated, and thoroughly dedicated, and he had outstanding credentials based on a track record of personal accomplishment. After he was removed from his job, he was broken and confused, but was still citing his impressive history and outstanding credentials. Then, in a final fit of frustration, he said: "If only business didn't have people in it, so much more could be accomplished."

Now for another example. "What is your career target?" an executive vice-president was asked. The answer: "I would like to be president of this company." The question: "Why do you want to be president?" The answer: "Because I feel that I can meet the enormous responsibilities of the job and that in that position I could best serve the company, its employees, stockholders, and various other publics."

This executive had some readily identifiable characteristics. He understood and believed in people and trusted them with as much responsibility as possible. As a direct result, his company had a positive climate characterized by mutual trust, faith, cooperation, respect, and confidence. He concentrated on developing his management team and surrounded himself with the strongest managers—each of whom could have been considered a potential back-up. He believed in integrity—his own and everyone else's—and insisted on honest, open communication from top to bottom and from bottom to top. As a result, everybody in the company felt free to tell it like it was. This president created a climate where individual freedom was balanced with the discipline of organization direction. Each person in the company knew his job and was dedicated to accomplishing its accountabilities and monitoring his own performance. Because people felt both secure and challenged, there was a low turnover. The policy of promoting primarily from within was made possible because of the growing, competent, self-reliant managers who blossomed in that rapidly—yet soundly—growing company. The company attracted and kept good people. This president believed his power was based primarily on the authority of earned prestige. He requested—he did not demand. Yet if there was a tough decision to be made and his management team could not reach a sound conclusion, he met his responsibility and made the decision. Because of his attitude, he received the enthusiastic, total support of his managers, even if they disagreed with him.

Power is frequently defined as "the possession of control, authority, or influence over others," while responsibility is defined as "the quality or state of being responsible, reliable, trustworthy." The paradox is that when a leader views his job in a context of responsibility, he attracts the power he needs to accomplish the job he feels should be done. On the other hand, regardless of how big and all-powerful his position, if a leader exercises power without responsibility, he will ultimately fail through lack of support from those on whom he depends for power (but doesn't know it). This principle applies equally to a president and a first-line manager.

Perhaps there really is no paradox here. Power and responsibility can be reconciled by a leader who understands that unless he establishes mutual trust, respect, and confidence—unless he believes in people—he probably will not, and should not, survive as a leader.

Granted, it is not always easy to be honest or meet the other demanding accountabilities of a leader. But to survive as a productive leader, it is necessary.

In Summation

As noted earlier, people and organizations that do not plan, manage, and influence their own future probably will not have one. In order to plan the future and pursue excellence, it is necessary to anticipate and manage change through the continuous application of a comprehensive system. The Planagement System has been designed to help you develop a sound plan for planning and management. It is grounded in the principle that the growth and development of an organization are directly dependent on the growth, development, and satisfaction of its people. In Planagement, the individual is the planning/management center with a primary purpose of seeing the best in others while giving the best he has.

Author's suggestion: In order to measure your understanding of the Planagement system, review and answer the questions on pages 3 and 4.

Part VI

Appendix
A Plan for Planning

Planning Function Plan Summary

PLANNING DATA

	THIS	REPLACES
FILE:	0.1	
DATE:	7/31/XX	
PAGE:	1 OF 2	OF

ORIGINATOR: Allen Ross, Planning Coordinator, Crescent Company

DISTRIBUTION: President and Planning Team

SUBJECT: Business/Function

A. Description of the Business
  1. *Definition:* This is a plan for the planning function of the Crescent Company.
  2. *Scope:*
     a. This plan is limited to the planning function and is based on the job description and accountabilities of the planning coordinator.
     b. The plan is for implementing the Planagement System throughout the Crescent Company and will include all people with other than routine responsibility and/or ambition.
  3. *Brief history:* The planning function was recently inaugurated in the Crescent Company primarily because of the rapid growth of the company and a growing need to establish a clear direction, proper priorities, improved profits, productivity, and control so as to achieve the desired results in a rapidly changing situation.
  4. *Flow diagram:*

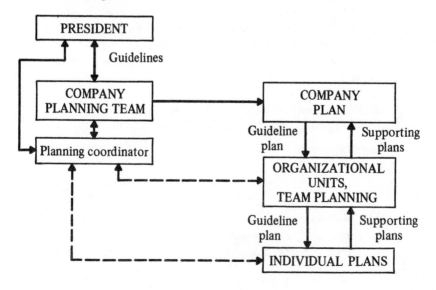

B. Mission
   1. To establish a company plan and the required supporting plans to make the company plan happen.
   2. To contribute to increasing the growth, profit, and profitability of the company, while increasing the growth, productivity, and satisfaction of its employees.
   3. To teach the planning skill to others.
   4. To become a professional general manager.

C. Nature of the Business
   1. Educationally oriented. Teach others to do the planning for their areas of responsibility.
   2. Employ superior skills in communication, coordination, and consolidation, as well as analysis and recommendations.
   3. This is a supportive, service-oriented type of function.

D. Unique Capabilities/Areas of Distinctive Competence/Available Resources/Skills
   1. *Unique capabilities:*
      a. Provides an overview of the entire company.
      b. Establishes a communications, coordination, and monitoring center.
   2. *Areas of distinctive competence:*
      a. Communicating.
      b. Thinking.
      c. Selling.
   3. *Available resources:*
      a. The Planagement System (provides a plan for planning).
      b. A sound company with an unlimited future.
      c. The allocation of time by the people participating in the program.
   4. *Skills:*
      a. Writing.
      b. Dealing well with people.
      c. Attention to detail while seeing the big picture.

E. Products/Services
   1. *Products:*

	Volume (% total)	Profit (% total)
a. The company plan	50%	Section 11
b. Supporting organizational unit plans	30%	Section 11
c. Individual supporting plans	20%	Section 11

184

Planning Function Plan Summary

PLANNING DATA

	THIS	REPLACES
FILE:	0.1	
DATE:	7/31/XX	
PAGE:	2 OF 2	OF

ORIGINATOR: Allen Ross, Planning Coordinator, Crescent Company
DISTRIBUTION: President and Planning Team
SUBJECT: Business/Function

E. Products/Services (Continued)
   2. *Services:*

	Volume (% total)	Profit (% total)
a. Teaching the system	60%	Section 11
b. Assisting in documentation	20%	Section 11
c. Consolidating, analyzing, reporting, and monitoring	20%	Section 11

F. Markets Served and Needs of These Served Markets
   (in order of importance)

Market	Need	Time Volume (% total)	Profit (% total)
1. President (CEO, COO function)	A company plan and control	20%	Section 11
2. Planning team	Coordination, consolidation effort	30%	Section 11
3. Organizational units	Supporting plans	30%	Section 11
4. Individual plans	Supporting plans	10%	Section 11
5. Planning function	Self-improvement	10%	Improved skill

Basically this is a marketing organization.

G. Customers Served and the Most Key Influences that Cause a Decision
   to Buy (in order of importance)

Customer	Key Influences
1. President	Understanding the process of planning and sound plans
2. Vice-presidents	Same
3. Department heads	Same
4. Individuals	Answer question, "What's in it for me?"

The key account approach is used.

185

H. Profit and/or Performance History (in order of importance)
   1. Company plan and performance of company—established Section 11.
   2. Supporting plans established.
   3. Exception report (% of total).
   4. Percent participation.
   5. Percent plans accomplished.

I. Present Organization
   1. See company organization chart.
   2. Planning coordinator reports to the president and coordinates with the company planning team.
   3. There is one committee—the Corporate Planning Committee—and it is chaired by the president. It has as its primary function to support the president's guidelines with a company plan and to keep the plan current through reporting by exception.
   4. The organization is marketing-oriented, with both functions and profit centers reporting to the president. The corporate planning team functions primarily as a communicating, coordinating, and consolidating unit in support of the president. The president is inclined to work alone and not through his planning team.
   5. The president founded the business, is very much of entrepreneur.

J. Accountabilities
   1. The title of the position is planning coordinator. There is no written position description.
   2.

Accountability	Acceptable Level of Performance	% of Time
a. Teaching the system	Individuals' understanding and continual use	25%
b. Company plan	Plan documented and current	25%
c. Supporting plans	Same	20%
d. Individual plans	Same	20%
e. Consolidation	Gap analysis and identification of key issues	10%

   3. The planning team, with the support of the planning coordinator, will be responsible for keeping the company plan current, updating once each month, or more often if required. The procedure to be followed is the exception reporting procedure (see Section 6 of the plan). The plan will be managed and kept current by the planning coordinator and will be submitted to the president and the planning team.
   4. All organizational units and people with other than routine responsibility and/or ambition will be included in this planning program.

	THIS	REPLACES
FILE:	0.2	
DATE:	7/31/XX	
PAGE:	1 OF 1	OF

PLANNING DATA

ORIGINATOR: Allen Ross

DISTRIBUTION: President and Planning Team

SUBJECT: Environment/Competition

A. <u>External Environment</u>
   (+) 1. Company is marketing-oriented and wants a supporting plan.
   (+) 2. There is a trend toward the behavioral sciences.
   (+) 3. A company planning team has been formed.
   (–) 4. People have a tendency to resist change and planning.
(+)(–) 5. Changes are very rapid.
   (–) 6. President is inclined not to work with his planning team.
B. <u>Internal Environment</u>
   (+) 1. Planagement System provides a plan for planning.
   (–) 2. There is a need for improved teaching and training skills by this planning coordinator.
   (+) 3. Confident that this program will be well received and successfully implemented.
   (–) 4. This is a new position and neither the position nor the function is understood.
   (–) 5. The president is reluctant to become involved with planning.
C. <u>Competition or Similar Operation</u>

	Name	Strength	Weakness	Strategy	Actions
1.	MBO	Widely known	Wrong focus Implementation	Use it as a component	Explain superior benefits of Planagement System
2.	Informal	Easier	People forget and are inconsistent	Show benefits of a formal system	Teach Planagement System support effort
3.	Time needed for operations	People feel comfortable when they are doing	May be doing the wrong thing or doing the thing wrong	Show benefits of planning	Answer question: What's in it for me?

D. Key Vulnerability
1. Human hang-ups and resistance to planning.
   Action: Teach people the system and show how it will benefit them directly.
2. Operating pressure on time.
   Action: Sell people on the benefits of making some time available for planning.
3. Paperwork requirement.
   Action: Reduce paperwork through the use of the exception report and support documentation efforts as required.

Planning Function Plan Summary

	THIS	REPLACES
FILE:	0.3	
DATE:	7/31/XX	
PAGE:	1 OF 1	OF

Originator: Allen Ross

Distribution: President and Planning Team

Subject: Capabilities/Opportunities/Alternative Actions

EVALUATION AND ANALYSIS

STRENGTHS/OPPORTUNITIES	WEAKNESSES/PROBLEMS	ACTION (Evolves Objectives)
Three Most Important Strengths	Three Most Important Related Weaknesses	Three Most Important Actions to be Taken
1. Planagement System provides a plan for planning. 2. President is behind the program. 3. Growing company with a recognized need for planning.	1. People's resistance to planning. 2. Lack of understanding of the Planagement System and the president has a tendency to work alone and not use his planning team. 3. People are very busy.	1. Teach people the system and emphasize the benefits to them. 2. Set up an introduction session and a two-day application with the planning team once the guidelines are obtained from the president. 3. Sell people on making needed time available.
Three Most Important Opportunities	Three Most Important Problems	Three Most Important Actions
1. To demonstrate how planning will contribute to increased growth, profit, and satisfaction.	1. Program is just starting and lacks a track record.	1. Carefully measure results of the planning effort and establish a recognized, respected track record.

(Form continues on reverse)

189

EVALUATION AND ANALYSIS (Continued)

STRENGTHS/OPPORTUNITIES	WEAKNESSES/PROBLEMS	ACTION (Evolves Objectives)
Three Most Important Opportunities	Three Most Important Problems	Three Most Important Actions
2. Identify the potential of the company and develop a plan to achieve it.	2. People are reluctant to spend time planning.	2. Make planning simple to understand, easy, rapid to apply, and measurable in the results achieved.
3. To earn a promotion through performance.	3. Reluctance to put a staff man in charge of a profit center. Weak in finance.	3. Develop skills required of a general manager and prove ability to perform in this role.

SUMMARY STATEMENT OF MOST IMPORTANT CAPABILITY, OPPORTUNITY, AND ACTION TO BE TAKEN

1. The prime capability is inherent in the Planagement System—a sound planning, management, control system that can be easily taught and applied.

2. There is an opportunity to contribute to improving the company's performance and therefore earn a promotion to general manager of a profit center—possibly a futures/ventures division.

3. The most important action is to successfully accomplish this plan and prepare myself to assume general manager's position.

190

Planning Function Plan Summary

PLANNING DATA

	THIS	REPLACES
FILE:	0.4	
DATE:	7/31/XX	
PAGE:	1 OF 1	OF

ORIGINATOR: Allen Ross

DISTRIBUTOR: President and Planning Team

SUBJECT: Assumptions/Potentials

A. Assumptions Made That Affect the Business and This Plan
   1. That the president and planning team will continue to support the planning effort and will approve this plan by 8/31/xx.
   2. That the needed time for sound planning will be made available as required.
   3. That there is a chance for me to become a general manager within this company.
   4. That the company has a much larger potential than is presently realized.
   5. That the company has the capability to grow soundly at a faster rate and improve its profits.
   6. That the Planagement System is as sound and productive as it appears to be.

B. Basic Assumptions Made Affecting Forecast and Key Objectives
   1. That key operating ratios will be used in support of the company plan.
   2. That this planning program will become a way of life and part of company policy and practice.

	THIS	REPLACES
FILE:	0.4C	
DATE:	7/31/XX	
PAGE:	1 OF 1	OF

COORDINATION REPORT

Originator: Allen Ross

Distribution: President and Planning Team

Subject: Assumptions Made for Support from Others

OBJECTIVE:

To gain approval of this plan by 8/31/xx.

(ASSUMPTIONS) (What, Who, When, Why)	SUPPORTING OBJECTIVE (What, Who, When)
That the president will review and approve this plan by 8/15/xx and submit it for review, approval, and support by the planning team by 8/31/xx.	Agreed: _____ President Agreed: (Planning Team Members) _____ _____ _____ _____ _____ _____

Confirmed by _____

Date _____

Dept. _____

	THIS	REPLACES
FILE:	0.4D	
DATE:	7/31/XX	
PAGE:	1 OF 1	OF

ORIGINATOR: Allen Ross

DISTRIBUTION: President and Planning Team

SUBJECT: Assumptions/Potentials

D. Potentials in Order of Priority, Including Their Estimated Value and the Actions Required to Achieve the Potential
  1. Increased profit and growth for the company and increased satisfaction and productivity for its employees. This is the most important potential because it will demonstrate the contribution that planning can make and my ability to help make it work. *Value:* See Section 11 of the Planagement plan for the company and compare it to present forecast, budget, and profit plan. *Action:* Develop the company plan by 12/15/xx and have it approved by 12/31/xx.
  2. To be promoted to general manager of the Futures Division. *Value:* Accomplishment of my career plan and ambition to become a general manager. *Action:* Prove my ability through the accomplishment of this plan, plus my self-development program, to gain the needed skills of a professional general manager.
  3. Personal growth in doing this job well. *Value:* This position is supportive to my desire to grow and become of more value. *Action:* Accomplish this plan and my plan for self-development and improvement.
  4. Teach people to use the Planagement skill so they will identify their potential and achieve more of it. *Value:* Increased satisfaction and productivity of people. *Action:* Establish a schedule for implementation that will include all employees with the company.

	THIS	REPLACES
FILE:	0.5	
DATE:	7/31/XX	
PAGE:	1 OF 1	OF

PLANNING DATA

ORIGINATOR: Allen Ross

DISTRIBUTION: President and Planning Team

SUBJECT: Objectives

A. Standard Objectives
   1. To gain approval of this plan by 8/31/xx.
   2. To gain approval of the company plan by 12/31/xx.
   3. To introduce the Planagement System to the planning team and develop a guideline company plan in two days, by 9/30/xx.
   4. To develop the organization unit supporting plans and the consolidated supporting plan to the company guideline plan by 11/30/xx.
   5. To present the gap analysis, overall analysis, consistency check, and key issues for decision to the planning team by 12/10/xx.
   6. To meet or exceed the forecast for this function.
      (See 0.5A6a)
B. Problem-Solving Objectives
   1. To have the planning responsibility made part of each person's job description by 1/31/xx + 1.
   2. To develop a written memo that spells out the benefits of the Planagement System as well as the anticipated results by 8/15/xx.
   3. To complete the formal introduction to the Planagement program by 9/15/xx.
   4. To complete a position description for this job by 10/1/xx.
C. Innovative Objectives
   1. To become general manager of the Futures Division by 12/31/xx + 3.
   2. To introduce at least one major improvement to the Planagement System each six months starting on 7/1/xx + 1.
   3. To complete my career plan and written program of self-development by 6/1/xx + 1.
D. Objectives in Support of Others
   (See 0.5D)
E. Most Important Objective in Each Key Result Area
   1. *Customer satisfaction:* By 12/31/xx + 1 to have people involved in the program consistently using it as measured by at least an x percent monthly exception report ratio.
   2. *Productivity:* By 9/1/xx + 1 to establish a method for measuring increased productivity on an individual job basis.
   3. *Innovation:* By 5/1/xx + 2 to develop and introduce an entrepreneurial salary administration program and gain approval of same.
   4. *Resources:* By 12/31/xx + 1 to have the assets employed in this business increased by at least x percent with a return on those assets of at least x percent before taxes.

5. *Management development and performance:* By 7/31/xx + 1 to introduce all people with other than routine responsibility and/or ambition to the system and have their completed written plans for their jobs.

6. *Employee attitudes and performance:* By 10/15/xx + 1 to contribute to converting the internal environment of the company to at least an x percent positive status.

7. *Public responsibility:* By 7/31/xx + 1 to have trained myself as a public speaker and have prepared a program that could be used by various community groups for better planning and achievement of potential.

8. *Communications:* By 6/1/xx + 1 to submit for approval a brochure that will enhance the image of the company by telling its story to its public·.

9. *Profitability:* By 7/31/xx + 1 to have clearly demonstrated through objective measurement the contribution that planning and implementation of the Planagement program has made to the company.

F. Most Important Objectives

0.5C1—to become general manager of the Futures Division by 12/31/xx + 3, and also (0.5A2) to gain approval of the company plan by 12/31/xx. These are my important objectives because in order to accomplish them, all other objectives in this plan will need to be successfully accomplished. In addition, these objectives unite my primary personal goal with the primary goal of the company, and 0.5A2 meets the president's guidelines.

G. Additional Objectives of Guideline Objectives That Must Be Supported

In the president's letter of 7/1/xx he stated he wants a completed and approved company plan by 12/31/xx.

PLANNING PROFILE

ORIGINATOR: Allen Ross
DISTRIBUTION: President, with copies to Planning Team
SUBJECT: Forecast (Annual and Long-Range)

FILE: 0.5A6a
DATE: 7/31/XX
PAGE: 1 OF 1

	HISTORICAL				CURRENT YR'	FUTURE				
	FOURTH YR.	THIRD YR.	SECOND YR.	LAST YR.	19xx	NEXT YR. 19xx + 1	SECOND YR. 19xx+2	THIRD YR. 19xx+3	FOURTH YR. 19xx + 4	FIFTH YR. 19xx+5
1 Completion and approval of company plan					12/31					
2 Completion of supporting plan					11/15					
3 Completion of consolidation					11/31					
4 Analysis and report					12/10					
5 Individual plans completed						7/31				
6 Exception reporting						2/1				
7 Futures Division plan approval								6/30		
8 Promotion to G.M. of Futures Division								12/31		
18										

197

	THIS	REPLACES
FILE:	0.5D	
DATE:	7/31/XX	
PAGE:	1 OF 1	OF

ORIGINATOR: Allen Ross

DISTRIBUTION: President and Planning Team

SUBJECT: Objectives in Support of Others

OBJECTIVE: President wants an approved company plan by 12/31/xx.

ASSUMPTIONS (What, Who, When, Why)	SUPPORTING OBJECTIVE (What, Who, When)
President assumes that a sound company plan can be developed by 12/31/xx and will require less than 20 percent of the key managers' time (including his), and he holds the planning coordinator responsible for accomplishing this objective. The reason he wants a plan is that he wants to establish a clear, long-term direction and priorities, and improve controls and profits through a better system of allocating and utilizing limited resources.	This plan supports the president's guideline, as established in his letter of 7/1/xx to me and the members of the planning team.

Confirmed Allen Ross

Date 7/31/xx

Dept. Planning Coordinator

Planning Function Plan Summary

PLANNING DATA

	THIS	REPLACES
FILE:	0.6	
DATE:	7/31/XX	
PAGE:	1 OF 2	OF

ORIGINATOR: Allen Ross

DISTRIBUTION: President and Planning Team

SUBJECT: Policies/Procedures/Strategy

A. Policies/Agreements/Procedures
   1. *Most important policies needed:*
      a. To make planning part of each person's job by adding as an accountability that he will submit a plan for his job within 60 days of having been assigned the job and will keep it current through exception reporting.
      b. The planning team will meet on the morning of the third Friday of each month.
      c. Each job will have a written position description.
   2. *Agreements or procedures that relate to the achievement of this plan:*
      a. See company *Procedure Manual* and include the procedures for exception reporting and for the coordination report.
      b. See Coordination Report Procedure in Section 6 of the supporting plan to this summary.
      c. See the Exception Reporting Procedure in Section 6 of the supporting plan to this summary.

B. Most Important Strategies for the Business and This Plan
   1. To make each person the planning/management/control center for his job.
   2. To use the Planagement System as our plan for planning.
   3. To work with the planning team on at least a once-a-month basis.
   4. To teach the Planagement System to others and eventually work myself out of this job and into the position of general manager of the Futures Division.
   5. To use the Planagement System to write a career plan and develop a self-development program.

C. Basic Strategy for Marketing, Products, Functions
   1. *Most important accountability:* Develop a program that will introduce the Planagement System and teach it through application so that the learning is the doing.
   2. *Most important market:* To have the president review and approve this plan.
   3. *Most important product:* To complete the company plan by concentrating on the president's guidelines and the consolidation of the supporting plans of those people reporting directly to the president.

C. Basic Strategy for Marketing, Products, Functions (Continued)
  4. *Most important customer:* Teach the president the system in a one-day application that will develop the initial guideline plan to be used in the two-day application session with the company planning team.

D. Key Strategy to Exploit the Most Important Capability, Opportunity, and Potential
  1. *Most important capability:* To use the Planagement System to start the planning program and then modify and tailor it as required rather than delay implementation by researching and developing a planning/management/control system.
  2. *Most important opportunity:* Compare the present forecast, budget, and profit plan with Section 11 of the Planagement plan and use this as a way to measure the benefit of this program and my ability to perform as a general manager.
  3. *Most important potential:* Use Section 11 of the company plan to measure this, as well as Section 2B on internal environment.

E. Key Strategy for the Most Important Objectives
  1. *Forecast:* Submit this plan for approval and support by the president and the planning team. Focus on the planning team for the implementation of the company plan.
  2. *Most important objective:* To successfully accomplish this plan as well as the plan I will establish for my career and program of self-development.
  3. *Key result areas:*
     a. Customer satisfaction: To include all people regardless of their position if they have more than routine ambition.
     b. Productivity: Establish in writing a defined way to measure productivity increases, the overall measurement to be based on the key ratios of sales and profit per employee and manager.
     c. Innovation: To use the Planagement salary administration approach.
     d. Resources: To establish key operating ratios as part of the company plan and to use this concept to control results and measure company growth.
     e. Management development and performance: To make planning part of each person's job, a policy of the company, and a way of life, as measured by continued use through exception reporting.
     f. Employee attitudes and performance: Have each employee complete the external and internal environment section of their plans for their jobs and for the company. Consider using an attitude survey or an individual profile analysis.
     g. Public responsibility: To offer my services to community groups, as time will permit and outside of business hours.
     h. Communications: To put the company's story in writing and provide it to the company's publics, including stockholders, employees, customers, suppliers, and community.

Planning Function Plan Summary

PLANNING DATA

	THIS	REPLACES
FILE:	0.6	
DATE:	7/31/XX	
PAGE:	2 OF 2	OF

ORIGINATOR: Allen Ross

DISTRIBUTION: President and Planning Team

SUBJECT: Policies/Procedures/Strategy

E. Key Strategy for the Most Important Objectives (Continued)
   3. *Key result areas: (Continued)*
      j. Profitability: To relate profitability to the company's potential
         rather than to the company's historic performance, and to
         identify this potential in Section 4 of the company plan and the
         gain in Section 11 of the company plan.

F. Strategy for Accomplishing the Most Important Objective and Obtaining
   the Most Important Potential
   To accomplish this plan and work in support of accomplishing the
   company plan, and to introduce such a rate of profit, growth, productivity, and satisfaction that the need for a Futures Division will become readily apparent, as will my qualifications to be its general
   manager.

PLANNING DATA

	THIS	REPLACES
FILE:	0.7	
DATE:	7/31/XX	
PAGE:	1 OF 1	OF

ORIGINATOR: Allen Ross

DISTRIBUTION: President and Planning Team

SUBJECT: Programs/Projections/Alternatives

A. Most Important Programs
1. Completion of the company plan. This is the primary guideline of the president and is, therefore, the most important objective of the planning function.
2. Review and approval of this plan by the president and the planning team.
3. Development of the president's guideline plan.
4. Development of the supporting plans to the president's guideline plan and then consolidating them into a supporting company plan to the president's guidelines.
5. Completion of the individual plans.
6. Development of a presentation teaching application program.

B. Additional Programs and Projects Required in Order to Achieve the Major Results-Oriented Business Accomplishments Expected from This Plan
1. Development and acceptance of needed policies and procedures.
2. Establishment of position descriptions.
3. Establishment of key operating ratios.
4. Establishment of my career plan and program of self-development.
5. Establishment of a structured program for introducing the Planagement System.

C. Key Alternatives
1. Limit its application to planning team members only.
2. Develop our own planning system instead of using the Planagement System.
3. Include the top three levels of management but no others.
4. Bring in a Planagement counselor to help us get the program started.

PLANNING DATA

Programs and Projects should be developed for each major action identified throughout the plan.

I. ACTION PROGRAM   Name and number: Company Plan—0.7A1

Approval of the company plan.

II. OBJECTIVE (What by When)   OBJECTIVE NUMBER 0.5A2

To gain approval of the company plan by 12/31/xx.

III. ASSUMPTION/POTENTIAL

1. This plan will be approved by both the president and the planning team by 8/31/xx.
2. The gains contributed by this planning program will be measurable and will be sufficient to attract all the needed support when required.

IV. STRATEGY (How, Approach)

To have the president use the Planagement System first in a one-day application, which will result in his written guideline plan, and then work with the planning team in a two-day application to develop a more detailed guideline plan and teach the method and prove its value at the same time.

A. Projects (Action Steps in Sequence)	B. Schedule (When)	C. Responsibility (Who)
1. Approval of this plan (Objective 0.5A1)	1. 8/31/xx	1. President and planning team
2. One-day application with president	2. 9/15/xx	2. President and me
3. Two-day application with planning team (0.5A3)	3. 9/30/xx	3. Planning team and me
4. Complete the supporting plans and consolidation (0.5A4)	4. 11/30/xx	4. Managers reporting to president and me
5. Analysis and report	5. 12/10/xx	5. Me to planning team and president
6. Approval of company plan	6. 12/31/xx	6. Planning team and president

V. RESOURCES REQUIRED

1. Money—within budget.
2. Manpower—90% of my time, 15% of the involved managers' time between now and 12/31/xx.
3. Materials/Other—The Planagement System, manuals, and other supporting techniques, tools, skills.

VI. COST/BENEFIT   PURPOSE/RESULTS (Why)

1. Cost is reflected by my budget and the time required by the people involved.
2. The president's guideline will be met and the company will increase its performance, as measured by Section 11 of the company plan.

VII. ALTERNATIVES CONSIDERED (Description and Disposition)

1. Work primarily with the president.
2. Be more of a planner than a teacher.

Planning Function Plan Summary

PLANNING DATA

	THIS	REPLACES
FILE:	0.7D1	
DATE:	7/31/XX	
PAGE:	1 OF 1	OF

Originator: Allen Ross

Distribution: President and Planning Team

SUBJECT: Planning and Implementing One Day at a Time

List the six most important actions you should accomplish tomorrow.

Action	Benefit/Result
1. Make an appointment with the president for review and approval of the plan.	1. To obtain president's approval, support, and participation.
2. Visit with at least two key members of the planning team to get their ideas on how the planning program should work.	2. Have the planning team feel they contributed to the program; use their ideas wherever possible.
3. Write out a format for developing a position description, using Section 1 of Planagement System as a guide.	3. To develop my own written position description and that of others as well.
4. Attend lunch at the Chamber of Commerce.	4. Tie into Planagement System to serve the community.
5. Prepare outline of program for presenting the Planagement System.	5. Need the best-structured introduction program that is possible.
6. Catch up on correspondence and complete report.	6. To handle the paperwork requirement of this job.

Put actions in order of importance and complete them one at a time.

1.	2
2.	1
3.	5
4.	3
5.	6
6.	4

OPERATIONAL SCHEDULE

Planning Function Plan Summary

	THIS	REPLACES
FILE:	0.8	
DATE:	7/31/XX	
PAGE:	1 OF 1	OF

ORIGINATOR: Allen Ross
DISTRIBUTION: President and Planning Team
SUBJECT: Most Important Objectives and Supporting Projects

In Order of Priority

Objectives and/or Projects	Number	July	Aug.	Sept.	Oct.	Nov.	Dec.	19xx+1 1	19xx+1 2	19xx+2	19xx+3	19xx+4	19xx+5
1 Approval of company plan	0.5F&A2						31						
2 Approval of planning function plan summary	0.5A1		31										
3 One-day application with president				15									
4 Planning team two-day application	0.5A3			30									
5 Complete supporting plans and consolidation	0.5A4					30							
6 Analysis and report							10						
7 General manager of Futures Division	0.5CI										12/31		

UNITS OF TIME
Year 19xx

Objectives and/or Projects	Number	Year 19xx								19xx + 1			19xx + 2	19xx + 3	19xx + 4	19xx + 5
		July	Aug.	Sept.	Oct.	Nov.	Dec.	1	2							
8 Complete all individual plans	Forecast 0.5A6								→7/31							
9 Exception reporting	0.5A6							→2/1								
10 Formal introduction program	0.5B3		→15													
11																
12																
13																
14																
15																
16																
17																
18																

207

	THIS	REPLACES
FILE:	0.9	
DATE:	7/31/XX	
PAGE:	1 OF 1	OF

ORIGINATOR: Allen Ross

DISTRIBUTION: President and Planning Team

SUBJECT: Organization/Delegation/Development

A. Present Organization Structure

The present organization structure is satisfactory to accomplish this plan.

B. Recommended Organization Changes to Accomplish the Plan

To have the president participate more with his planning team.

C. Projected Organization Chart for the Next Five Years

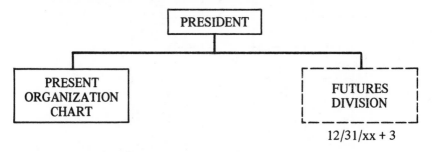

12/31/xx + 3

D. Manpower Requirements and Plan for the Next Five Years

Establishment of a back-up to the planning coordinator by 12/31/xx + 2.

E. Development Program for Self, Company, and People Reporting to Me

1. *Self-development program:* Reach Objective 0.5C3 in career plan and program of self-development by 5/1/xx + 1.

2. *Company's development program:* Implementation of the Planagement System throughout the company.

3. *Subordinates' development program:* Not applicable.

	THIS	REPLACES
FILE:	0.10	
DATE:	7/31/XX	
PAGE:	1 OF 1	OF

ORIGINATOR: Allen Ross

DISTRIBUTION: President and Planning Team

SUBJECT: Budget/Resources

A.–F. Financial Statements
See budget for this function in Section 10 of the supporting plan to this summary.

H.   Additional Major Resources Required to Accomplish This Plan
1. Participation of the president and the planning team and at least 15 percent of their time between now and 12/31/xx.
2. Approval of this plan by 8/31/xx.

	THIS	REPLACES
FILE:	0.11	
DATE:	7/31/XX	
PAGE:	1 OF 1	OF

ORIGINATOR: Allen Ross

DISTRIBUTION: President and Planning Team

SUBJECT: Justification/Results/Profitability

A, B, and D. <u>Most Important Gains (Results) to Be Achieved from This Plan</u>
1. The president's guideline will be successfully met.
2. The company's profit and growth will be measurably increased, as shown in Section 11 of the company plan.
3. My personal career plan will be achieved.
4. A more positive company climate and increased satisfaction and individual productivity will be achieved.
5. The company will identify and achieve more of its potential.

C. <u>Key Recommendations and Their Justification for Approval</u>
1. That this plan be approved no later than 8/31/xx by both the president and the planning team.

EXCEPTION REPORT

Originator: Allen Ross   Area: Planning   Date: 7/31/xx

Distribution: President and Planning Team'   File: 12.1

Copies (Others Affected):

REFERENCE: REVISED EXECUTIVE SUMMARY SECTION(S) ATTACHED AS CIRCLED .1 .2 .3 .4 ⑤ .6 .7 ⑧ .9 .10 .11

REFERENCE (OBJECTIVE NO., FUNCTION OR PRODUCT PLAN NAME):

Planning Function Plan

I. NATURE OF CHANGE(S) AND CAUSE FOR THE CHANGE(S) PRESENT AND/OR ANTICIPATED: 1. NATURE OF BUSINESS/ FUNCTION. 2. ENVIRONMENT/COMPETITION. 3. CAPABILITIES/OPPORTUNITIES. 4. ASSUMPTIONS/POTENTIALS.

This plan is not approved until 9/30/xx due to press of business.

II. MAJOR NEEDS, PROBLEMS, ADVANTAGES, OPPORTUNITIES CAUSED BY CHANGE (PRESENT AND/OR ANTICIPATED).

III. ADJUSTMENTS TO BE MADE AND RESULTS EXPECTED: 5. OBJECTIVES/GOALS. 6. POLICIES/PROCEDURES/STRATEGY. 7. PROGRAMS/PROJECTS/ALTERNATIVES. 8. PRIORITIES/SCHEDULES. 9. ORGANIZATION/DELEGATION/DEVELOPMENT. 10. BUDGETS/RESOURCES. 11. JUSTIFICATION(S).

President's guideline cannot be met because the company plan will not be approved until 1/31/xx + 1 because of the 30-day delay.

(Form continues on reverse)

IV. IMPACT OF CHANGE ON OBJECTIVE(S)—I.E., FORECAST/ACTUAL. 5. RESTATEMENT OF OBJECTIVE(S).

Most important objective is delayed by 30 days.

Approved by .... Date ....

V. SUMMARY. (CHECK ONE AND INCLUDE COMMENTS AND/OR ATTACHMENTS AS REQUIRED.)

A. ☒ Off Plan (See above and required attachment(s).)

B. ☐ On Plan (No change(s); this form complete if this box is checked.)

C. ☐ Plan Changed

Submitted by .... **Allen Ross** ....

Position .... **Planning Coordinator**

212

Selected Bibliography

Allen, Louis A., *The Management Profession*. New York: McGraw-Hill, 1964.
Batten, Joe D., *Tough-Minded Management*. New York: AMACOM, 1963.
———, *Beyond Management by Objectives*. New York: AMACOM, 1966.
Drucker, Peter F., *The Practice of Management*. New York: Harper & Row, 1954.
———, *The Effective Executive*. New York: Harper & Row, 1967.
Ewing, David W., *The Human Side of Planning*. New York: The Macmillan Company, 1969.
Kepner, Charles H., and B. B. Tregoe, *The Rational Manager*. New York: McGraw-Hill, 1965.
Koontz, Harold, and Cyril O'Donnell, *Principles of Management*. 5th ed. New York: McGraw-Hill, 1972.
Maltz, Maxwell, *Psycho-Cybernetics: The New Way to a Successful Life*. Englewood Cliffs, N.J.: Prentice-Hall, 1960.
McGregor, Douglas, *The Human Side of Enterprise*. New York: McGraw-Hill, 1960.
———, *The Professional Manager*. New York: McGraw-Hill, 1967.
Odiorne, George S., *Management by Objectives: A System of Managerial Leadership*. New York: Pitman Publishing Corp., 1965.
Sampson, Robert C., *Managing the Managers: A Realistic Approach to Applying the Behavioral Sciences*. New York: McGraw-Hill, 1965.
Steiner, George A., *Top Management Planning*. New York: The Macmillan Company, 1969.
Toffler, Alvin, *Future Shock*. New York: Random House, 1970.
Townsend, Robert, *Up the Organization*. New York: Alfred A. Knopf, 1970.

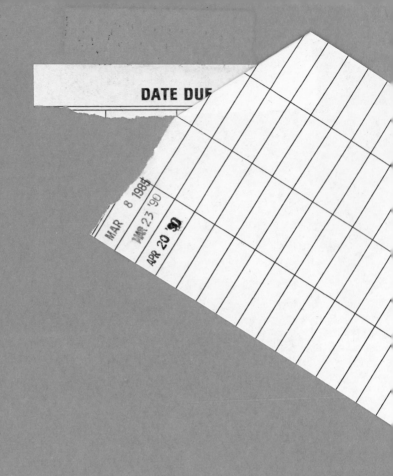

DATE DUE

MAR 8 1985
MAR 23 '90
APR 20 '90